Media, Sound, & Culture

in Latin America and the Caribbean

Edited by Alejandra Bronfman & Andrew Grant Wood

UNIVERSITY OF PITTSBURGH PRESS

Published by the University of Pittsburgh Press, Pittsburgh, Pa., 15260
Copyright © 2012, University of Pittsburgh Press
All rights reserved
Manufactured in the United States of America
Printed on acid-free paper
10 9 8 7 6 5 4 3 2 1

Library of Congress Cataloging-in-Publication Data

Media, sound, and culture in Latin America and the Caribbean / edited by Alejandra
Bronfman and Andrew Grant Wood.
p. cm. — (Pitt Latin American series)
Includes bibliographical references and index.
ISBN 978-0-8229-6187-1 (pbk. : acid-free paper)
1. Mass media and culture—Latin America. 2. Mass media and culture—Caribbean
Area. 3. Sound in mass media. 4. Radio broadcasting—Latin America. 5. Radio broadcasting—Caribbean Area. I. Bronfman, Alejandra, 1962– II. Wood, Andrew Grant,
1958–
P94.65.L29M44 2012
302.23098—dc23   2011048868

Media, Sound, & Culture
in Latin America and the Caribbean

Pitt Latin American Series

John Charles Chasteen and Catherine M. Conaghan, Editors

For my students, who make me think, and Maia and
Nina, who fill my life with terrific noise.

In memory of our dear colleague Adrian Bantjes, and for my new friends
in Tulsa who have taught me how to listen from the heart.

CONTENTS

INTRODUCTION

Media, Sound, and Culture

Alejandra Bronfman & Andrew Grant Wood

> *Every time I see the sun rise*
> *Or a mountain that's so high*
> *Just by seeing is believing*
> *I don't need to question why*
> *When I see a mighty ocean*
> *That rushes to the shore.*
>
> —Elvis Presley, "Seeing Is Believing"

> *For twenty-five centuries, western knowledge has tried to look upon the*
> *world. It has failed to understand that the world is not for beholding. It is for*
> *hearing. It is not legible, but audible.*
>
> —Jacques Attali, *Noise*

Is THE WORLD for seeing and believing, as Elvis Presley once put it, or for hearing, as Jacques Attali's provocative statement alleges? Of course, a narrow choice between seeing and hearing is unnecessary, since our prevailing epistemological paradigm allows for a wide range of sensory information in determining what we think we know. Nevertheless, for most people, vision has enjoyed a privileged status in Western civilization since the Renaissance, if not before. In turn, this prejudice has relegated the other senses—including hearing—to a marginal role in our philosophical and literary pursuits.

This book contends, however, that soundscapes, music, noise, and silence all reveal to us something about prevailing worldviews, technologies, epistemologies, and aspirations past and present. For the most part, we agree with Attali when he asserts "our sight has dimmed," but we'd like to phrase it differently: our hearing has dulled. Conversely, Attali implores us to listen and find ways to take more seriously the importance of sound as a social artifact. This seems particularly relevant at the moment, when we bear witness to a constant barrage of images, signs, and television and computer screens in our present neoliberal age, and hyper-commodification rules the day with its proclivity for flash, glitter, and profit-driven spectacle. Perhaps our sight has not dimmed so much as become overstimulated. In any case, as historians, we find Attali's charge that "we must learn to judge a society more by its sounds, by its art, and by its festivals, than by its statistics" compelling.[1]

Much has happened, however, since Attali first published *Noise* in 1977. The dawning and initial flowering of our present digital age has provided the technological means for much positive innovation in the recording, mixing, and propagation of sound. At its most basic, sound requires a medium to transmit it. This medium is that of countless, elastic air particles that resonate once an initial energy force gives rise to the vibration we identify as a sound wave.[2] Once amplified, broadcast, and/or recorded, the study of sound then becomes inextricably tied to the study of media. It is precisely this realm that has undergone a complete transformation. With the advent of the Internet, sound has become associated with new forms of power, such as transnational production, and media has fostered faster, more individualistic, more globalized practices of consumption.

Yet, sound and listening, as well as the technologies and media that make them possible, are too easily taken for granted in our understanding of the present and the past. In fact, sound is produced in particular historical settings, supported by networks of power and money, and subject to contingency and contestation. In other words, it is not only cultural but also political. Who gets to make noise, who must remain silent, who is heard, and who is ignored? Who determines what counts as legitimate sound and what is rendered as mere noise? What particular voices and sounds are deemed important, proper, or appealing, and why are others deemed antisocial? These are distinctions that permeate our everyday lives today, just as they did in the past. By offering a sampling from a wide range of places and times, our intention in this book is to build upon

Attali's challenge in privileging sound as *a critical sense* in which to decipher issues of social and cultural change.

Of course, we are not alone in calling for a move away from the spectatory, visually dominant study of the past toward an expanded, full-sensory approach to history. Drawing inspiration from the notion of the soundscape—the sonic environment—as elaborated by R. Murray Schafer, scholars such as Alain Corbin and David Cressy studied the regulation of space and time through aural markers such as bells.[3] Leigh Eric Schmidt, Richard Cullen Rath, and Mark Smith produced rich explorations of the soundscapes of the eighteenth- and nineteenth-century United States arguing for the sonic dimensions of religion, nature, or slavery.[4] Turning to the relationship between sound and technology, Jonathan Sterne and Emily Thompson attended to the origins of recorded sound and the engineering of acoustic environments, respectively, with compelling claims about the sound of modernity.[5] Although this limited list focuses on North American soundscapes, sound studies spans the globe and includes scholars such as Charles Hirschkind, who has analyzed cassette sermons, listening practices, and affective spirituality in Egypt; Kevin Birth, who has listened to Carnival and politics in Trinidad; and Michael Veal, whose work has traced the social and technological origins of "dub" in Jamaica.[6]

Scholars of Latin America and the Caribbean have been particularly interested in electronic mass communications media of the twentieth and early twenty-first centuries, including radio, film, and television. The work of Reynaldo González, Inés Cornejo, Portugal Rubén Gallo, and Guillermo Mastrini, to name just a few, has inquired into the ways that technology and the infrastructure of communication shape everyday life and contribute to political outcomes.[7] As Bryan McCann and Sergio Arribá have demonstrated, key political styles such as populism would not have been possible without the microphone or the radio.[8] Moreover, scholars such as Oscar Luis López, Joy Hayes, and Robert Claxton have argued for the significance of the media to the constituted boundaries of nation.[9]

As historians of Latin America and the Caribbean, we find, despite these contributions, continuing silences in the relationship of sound to history.[10] With this we ask: what are/have been the sounds of the region, and how can we understand them as embedded in and revealing of larger social and cultural meanings? One of the answers has almost become a cliché: Latin America and the Caribbean are known for their music, if nothing else. In some ways we know a great deal about sound in this part of the world, as the histories of the tango, samba, bolero, son, mambo, and vallenato have demonstrated the power of music to build identities and communities, to bring new value to the recently excoriated, to bring fame and wealth to select musicians, and to carve out spaces of specificity in an increasingly globalized commercial marketplace.[11]

Nevertheless, music has practically drowned out other Latin American and Caribbean sounds. The chapters presented in this book move beyond music to soundscapes that resonate with countless commercial jingles and advertising slogans, to anthems and speeches rife with political propaganda, and to earsplitting fireworks explosions at local festivals. When the authors of these chapters do include music in their analysis, they are especially attentive to the broader contexts of record or broadcast production and the networks that ultimately disseminated them. This edited volume aims to decenter music in the study of Latin American and Caribbean sound, not by excluding it altogether but by including it as part of a multivocal sonic environment.

Moreover, many of the authors take on the challenge of reception—listening. Significantly, they heed the material nature of networks, taking into account unevenness and contingencies. Further, they acknowledge resistance to media hegemony upon reception and factor it into a more subtle interpretation of media discourses and practices. The work of Jesus Martín-Barbero is key here, as he suggests that it is precisely the mediating dynamic that ought not be overlooked in efforts to understand the power of mass communication and people's responses to it.[12] Listeners do not necessarily relinquish agency when they listen; they hear selectively. The contributions that follow take this as a point of departure in their precisely observed explorations of the aural.

Bringing together often disparate literatures, this edited volume puts the study of Latin America and the Caribbean in conversation, so to speak, with the study of sound and the media. Building on the convergence of fields, the contributors attend to the social and cultural meanings of sound and the practices of listening. This approach opens up new methodologies and extends the boundaries of scholarly inquiry. One of the main challenges in the study of sound is locating sources in which the traces of past sounds reside. This is an epistemological puzzle that requires a rethinking of our approach to sources.[13] The contributors have read texts after the manner of conventional scholarship, but they have also sought to hear whatever they could in the documentation. Sometimes, this involved reading texts for particular sounds. Sometimes, this involved listening to recordings, cautiously upstreaming from more contemporary ethnographic accounts. Moreover, the contributors have worked to glean what Roland Barthes has called "the grain of the voice" from these texts or recordings—not just the words spoken but also how they were spoken and by whom, not just who listened but also how they heard.[14]

The diverse range of sound cultures in Latin American and Caribbean history requires us to pay close attention to specific geographic, social, and technological configurations and distinctions across time and space. Approaching selected topics in the aural history of the region by way of a variety of different methods, the chapters in this collection divide along three main themes: appreciating the relationship of sound to writing and authorship, as well as considering the act of listening as a bodily/disembodied practice; assessing the critical relationships among media, technology, and politics; and understanding the process by which sounds create and contest identities and boundaries in public celebrations.

Part I: Embodied Sounds and the Sounds of Memory

Fernando de Sousa Rocha's chapter "Recovering Voices: The Popular Music Ear in Late Nineteenth- and Early Twentieth-Century Brazil" proposes that we examine listening to popular music in relation to oral and print cultures. In this, he analyzes the diverse conjunctions between orality and writing within different examples of Brazilian popular music. Among some of the questions he considers, de Sousa Rocha asks how listening is informed by notions of style or authorship and how—along the continuum between public and private spheres—listening helps to forge social distinctions.

Christine Ehrick's "Radio Transvestism and the Gendered Soundscape in Buenos Aires, 1930s–1940s" considers early radio in the Río de la Plata as a site where gender, citizenship, and the public sphere were contested and reconstituted. Raising intriguing theoretical questions about the relationship between the voice and the body, Ehrick interrogates the idea that radio speech is "disembodied," instead arguing that the human voice is inherently corporeal. Further, she charges that radio vocalizations represent a projection and performance of the body in an exclusively sonic way, which in turn highlights the fact that the voice is critical in coding the body along presumed racial, class, and gendered lines. Together, the chapters in part I raise questions about the ways in which the sounds of voices are recorded and remembered and about the meanings such sounds take on in a range of contexts. They also open new methodological possibilities for studying relationships among bodies, technologies, and power.

Part II: The Media of Politics

Gisela Cramer's "How to Do Things with Waves: United States Radio and Latin America in the Times of the Good Neighbor" traces the relationship between the United States and Latin America during the late 1930s and early 1940s when broadcasting content changed markedly across the hemisphere. During the early years of World War II, Latin America gained a presence never before enjoyed on U.S. airwaves, and many programs rather explicitly sought to instill sympathy with and respect for the region's culture, history, and civilization. Rather than treating this episode simply as yet another facet of the Good Neighbor policy, Cramer carefully considers the workings of Good Neighbor Radio as a construction site for an *imagined community* on a larger, pan-American scale.

Alejandra Bronfman's "Weapons of the Geek: Romantic Narratives, Sonic Technologies, and Tinkerers in 1930s Santiago, Cuba" uses three different episodes to argue for the political significance of sonic technologies and of people with the knowledge to repair or maintain them. In each case, both repertoires of contention and strategies of surveillance depended on the ability to control the transmission of information with sound. This chapter also engages romantic narratives about the power of sound, inquiring as to the ways these narratives served as scripts for the actors involved. Bronfman suggests that the promise of freedom through sonic technologies became the premise for greater surveillance, once law enforcement realized that new capacities also meant new vulnerabilities.

Alejandro L. Madrid's "Music, Media Spectacle, and the Idea of Democracy: The Case of DJ Kermit's 'Góber'" follows the curious tale that originated with a Mexican media broadcast of a telephone conversation between Mario Marin, the governor of Puebla, and Kamel Nacif, an influential businessman linked to international child pornography and prostitution networks. The recording confirmed the complicity of the governor in kidnapping and trying to illegally imprison Lydia Cacho, the journalist who had publicly revealed Nacif's connections to child pornography. The broadcast of the conversation ignited a media frenzy that revealed the practices of corruption, misogyny, and censorship prevalent in the Mexican political system, but it also put in evidence the media's commodification of ideas such as democracy and freedom in an attempt to increase ratings. The attention to sonic media and its explicit relationship to political strategies in each of these chapters offer new ways to explore politics and technology in Latin America.

Part III: The Sonics of Public Spaces

Gonzalo Araoz's "Alba: Musical Temporality in the Carnival of Oruro, Bolivia" asserts that rhythm and memory are highly relevant concepts to explain the complex phenomenon of temporal perception in relation to the celebration of Carnival in the Bolivian city of Oruro. Araoz focuses on the cacophonous performance of the Alba rite in the Oruro Carnival, where dozens of brass bands perform different Morenada tunes simultaneously, giving rise to a peculiar sense of time and memory of time. Araoz argues that the sonic chaos of the Alba rite demands an approach that considers both musical and temporal dimensions and points to the the relevance of the philosopher of music Victor Zuckerkandl. According to Zuckerkandl the feeling of rhythm is the experience (or even the cognition) of time itself. This is crucial to understanding temporal perception during the Alba rite in Oruro, when the notions of pause, repetition, time, and memory are often musically blurred together.

Andrew Grant Wood's "Such a Noise! Fireworks and the Soundscapes of Two Veracruz Festivals" compares the use of fireworks during two annual public celebrations in the Mexican state of Veracruz: Carnival in the modern, industrial port of Veracruz and Candelaria in the river town of Tlacotalpan. Tracing the historical deployment of fireworks in Veracruz, Wood notes how pyrotechnics have long been used to mark festival time and space. Observing the acoustic history of each of these undertakings with a special interest in fireworks, he then examines how fireworks play an essential role in the process of community self-identification, promotion, and life-affirming reflection. These two noisy contributions are a fitting ending to this book, which aims to remind readers to pay attention to the din and clatter of the Latin American past and present. And finally, Michele Hilmes's generous postscript indicates future possibilities for our collective endeavors.

If, given the technological capacities of computer software and cinematic special effects, seeing is no longer believing, perhaps one can say that the same is also true of sound. Torn from the context of its production and reverberating through time and space, sound can persuade or deceive as easily as visual images. Nevertheless, this does not mean that sound should not or cannot be studied. Indeed, as many of the chapters in this book suggest, what is interesting is precisely the processes by which sound is generated, duplicated, amplified, altered, and propagated. If we are subject to an abundance of images, so too are we subject to a multiplicity of sounds—voices, machines, animals, and the landscape itself all make noise—that merit attention. Our continued epistemological overreliance on the spectatory in researching and writing about the past puts us at risk. If sight remains the primary sense by which we constitute and represent our scholarship, then we have marginalized much that is relevant to other sense records potentially rich in information and cultural clues. Sound (both natural and mediated) offers us much in the way of content. It can inform us about historical qualities related to time and space. In human terms, it has the ability to reveal personal emotions, moods, and messages. Sound, in other words, is rich in potential meaning if we are willing to listen.

This is a call for new histories of Latin America and the Caribbean significantly informed by sound but also, ultimately, by *all possible senses* and not just those exclusively rooted in sight and text-based documentation. What follows is by no means a comprehensive collection of "sound histories" but a pioneering aural source sampling. In this, we hope to encourage further explorations and experimentations leading, perhaps, to a methodological renaissance of sorts—one that rejoins the sensory with the epistemological in thinking about the past.

Media, Sound, & Culture
in Latin America and the Caribbean

Embodied Sounds and the
Sounds of Memory

RECOVERING VOICES

The Popular Music Ear in Late Nineteenth- and Early Twentieth-Century Brazil

Fernando de Sousa Rocha

Como podia acontecer aquela voz? Ela era ninguém, só podia usar silêncios.
—Mia Couto "O apocalipse privado do tio Geguê,"
Cada homem é uma raça

SINCE ITS VERY beginning, recording has been closely related to writing. From a representation of sounds with marks or written letters, the term phonograph easily came to represent an imaginary machine that could record sounds and, later, Thomas Edison's invention. The slippage in mean--ing is based on a fundamental common trait; in both cases, an inscription produces a reusable object. That such a production should define recording techniques is of the utmost importance because it alters the manner in which we listen. In markedly oral cultures, the act of listening is necessarily tied to the moment of sound production and is therefore situated. However, this should not suggest that we need to establish a clear-cut distinction, when analyzing sound cultures in Latin America, between nonmediated and technologically mediated sonic events. My objective is not to establish a clear-cut development from orality to writing, or from a non-media-based to a media-based culture. On the contrary, I would like to analyze the diverse conjunctions between the two aforementioned

3

modes of communication within different instances of producing and listening to popular music, and I focus on late nineteenth- to early twentieth-century Brazil.

As Murray Schafer proposes, written accounts are often the only documents we have available in order to investigate sound (re)production and reception prior to the development of sound recording technology.[1] Nevertheless, one should not overlook the fact that writing itself is a sound recording technology, which is applied to both language and musical notation. To a certain extent, issues related to the mastery and control over sound recording and transmission through writing are transferred to modern sound recording and transmitting technologies, albeit in always modified forms. In this sense, texts that focus on how orally based cultures are exposed to writing allow us to inquire about the status of sound recording and reproducing technologies in Latin America. Within this context, "Carta canta" (A Letter Sings), by Peruvian writer Ricardo Palma (1833–1919), is an exemplary narrative in that it demonstrates how sound recording technology often excludes certain subjects as speakers, only to register their voices as the recording subject hears them.[2] Lacking a say in recorded speech, these subjects are, in this sense, spectral voices, bearing a presence similar to the ghostly matters that Avery F. Gordon seeks to render evident as she paradoxically tracks "through time and across forces that which makes its mark by being there and not there at the same time."[3] What is thus encapsulated in the expression "Carta canta," which gives title to Palma's story, is an experiential knowledge resonating through a voice that is never quite there.

Uncovering such ghostly voices leads us to a multiplicity of texts that further explore the issues contained in Palma's narrative, such as the novel *Triste fim de Policarpo Quaresma* (The patriot; 1915), by Lima Barreto (1881–1922), and the short story "Um homem célebre" (A celebrity; 1888), by Machado de Assis (1839–1908). Both narratives deal with popular music and sound (re)production, and thus I resort to them—as well as to other auxiliary texts and songs—in order to explore which issues we face if we are to recover those voices that have remained barely audible in the process of sound recording. First of all, one must recognize that, regarding sound recording, even when one hears a voice, one is never in the presence of a single voice, for it responds to and interpolates so many other voices. As a scene in the novel *Triste fim de Policarpo Quaresma* suggests, we are always dealing with superposed voices.[4] Singers and speakers always embody

other voices, which may sound like a polyphonic piece or an oral palimpsest in which certain voices are recorded over others. Such erasure of voices
is particularly at work once authorial names come to play a decisive part in
the production and consumption of popular music. However, precisely because authorship appears to gather disparate voices under one name, there
remains a certain anxiety binding the author's name to popular music, as
we see in Machado de Assis's "Um homem célebre," for oral-aural reproduction tends to wipe out authorial names.[5] Technological development,
such as that brought about by telephones and phonographs, would only
hasten the disembodiment implicit in sound (re)production without ever
eroding, to its fullest extent, the desire for a presence that would give a *corpus,* an origin, to the voices we hear.

Ghostly Voices

Ricardo Palma's renowned "Carta canta" tells the story of two Indians
who are in charge of taking ten melons from a farm in Barranca to their
master's home in Lima. Together with the fruit, the steward hands them
a letter, also to be given to the master, don Antonio Solar. Curious about
the fruit's taste (they had never tried melon), the Indians eat two of the
fruit, but not before they hide the letter. They believe that, if the letter sees
them eating, it will tell on them. Needless to say, the master discovers their
deed—given that the letter states exactly how many melons he should
receive—and punishes them accordingly. "¡Carta canta!"—such is the
Indians' conclusion in Palma's *tradición.*[6] Their recognition that the letter
speaks (literally, sings) reinforces both their own perspective on recording and the master's authority. In the end, don Antonio reiterates what the
Indians had already deduced on their own, using the Indians' "ignorance"
to his advantage. Yelling that they know now that letters speak while ad-
monishing them to be more careful next time, don Antonio warns the
Indians against the power of writing, a power that favors him and reinforces the rights and power structures that had already been sanctioned
orally. As the narrator observes, not long before, an oral refrain had the
same value as an aphorism or an article in the constitution. When don Antonio supposedly writes on a wall "Al que me echare de mi casa y hacienda,
yo lo echaré del mundo," he only restates, in writing, what the oral refrain
had already asserted.[7] Writing, in this context, is always a posteriori, a recording of that which is already known.

What is not made explicit in that recording of voices is that many subjects, as users, may be "thrown out" of a certain technological realm. According to the narrator, the Indians are "ignorant" of writing. However, they feel in it "a diabolical and marvelous power" and believe "not that the letters were conventional signs, but spirits, that not only functioned as messengers but also as lookouts or spies."[8] Having no mastery over writing, the Indians cannot fully comprehend how writing works, as a sound recording system, and they are quite right in seeing such foreign technology as a watchman or spy of sorts, relaying messages, which they cannot decode, from one literate man to another. With their own explanation of writing to guide them, the Indians no longer face an encounter with an Other but rather a network—a discursive, mediating apparatus that is still effective nowadays. If one may speak of "ignorance" in Palma's tale, as the narrator suggests, it can only refer to the Indians' supposition that, in order to speak, the spirit-letter would first have to see. As we know, don Antonio's ability to uncover their actions proves them wrong. However, their mistake is shortly followed by an amazing insight: "¡Carta canta!" At no point in the text does the master read the letter aloud, giving voice to the spirit-letter. He simply reiterates what the steward had stated in the letter, and, because of its truthfulness to facts, the Indians know that the spirit-letter witnesses without seeing and speaks without voicing. Lacking the skills to utilize the writing/reading technology, the Indians are not, by the end of the episode with the melons, ignorant of writing at all. They know that letters need no presence or voice to speak or sing—only their own diabolical spirit—and thus they enter the field of power by means of a cultural translation, an incomprehension that means comprehending rightly enough.

In the long run, "writing, the letter of the law, which sees it all and tells it all, occupies the native subject's subjectivity," which the narrative itself recovers.[9] Were it not for writing, even when it supports relations of power and domination, what would we be able to hear now of the Indians' voices? Could these subaltern subjects find a manner of contradicting power other than learning how to pose a threat in the future tense, as don Antonio did, anonymously? In order to find an answer to this question, we must hear ghostly voices, recorded in writing against the author's hands: "¡Carta, canta!" Rather than accept that writing speaks (though silently), one must revert it to voice. Such a process, which became possible only once it also became possible to record any type of sound, allowed us, to a certain extent, to bypass writing, at least from the consumers' point of view. In the specific case of Brazil, with its high illiteracy rates when sound recording technology began to be commercialized, it would seem that Brazilians immersed in a secondary type of orality. This does not mean to say that, with new sound recording technology, we may skirt the issues that the story of the stolen fruit so clearly exposes. Rather, these issues reappear in different manners and respond to the specificities that new media impose on users, including the renovated relationships between oral sound production and writing/print cultures.

Oral Palimpsests

Until the invention of electric recording, soft voices could be not picked up and registered, and so the very first recordings by Casa Edison—the most important recording company in early twentieth-century Brazil—favored either singers with a strong voice volume or bands based on wind instruments, such as Banda do Corpo de Bombeiros or Casa Edison's own band. Songs were often recorded only as instrumental pieces, and the lyrics were to be learned either through listening or by memorizing written or printed copies. Playing these songs, listeners performed the same type of ventriloquism that characterized writing, reconverting the voice that had been inscribed in the written text—which, in the case of early recordings, remained implicit and unsung but ready to be actualized—back to its oral-aural nature. Even more clearly than the songs, these instrumental pieces expose the relationship between listener and singer. Like a reader, such as don Antonio in "Carta canta," the listener blends his or her voice with another—namely, that of the speaker/singer who may not be present but who is certainly heard, albeit through a different voice.

What sound recording technologies allow for, as when don Antonio reads the letter or when someone places a record on a gramophone, is a palimpsest of voices, which one may hear in the actualized voice of the speaker or singer. However, not all of these voices have been preserved. Given the initial difficulty of finding materials and a process that would result in lasting recordings, sound became incomprehensible after some time, and both cylinders and records were then scraped in order to be reutilized. From its inception, modern sound recording technology functioned as a material metaphor for oral palimpsests, raising the question of how many (and whose) voices one may hear and which ones are ultimately scraped off the records. Letters, cylinders, and records—operating as media in place of an "original" voice—reconfigure the in-person situation in which the speaker or singer lends his or her voice to another.

In his novel *Triste fim de Policarpo Quaresma*, Lima Barreto succinctly describes an episode that exemplifies how different voices, coming from different sources, are called to speaking. The scene begins when the musician Ricardo Coração dos Outros, tormented by a competitor's rising popularity, laments that his ungrateful homeland does not appreciate his efforts to publicize the most Brazilian of all music forms, *modinhas*, and its most faithful musical instrument, the guitar. Nevertheless, all are indifferent to his suffering, and he has no lover or friend to receive his tears that fall on the ground. Lonely, Ricardo recalls a verse: "If I weep . . . the scorching sand drinks my tears."[10] The verse comes from "Vozes d'África" (Voices of Africa; 1868), by Romantic poet Castro Alves (1847–1871). In this poem, the African continent, impersonated as a woman, addresses God and complains about its fate. With that verse in mind, Ricardo lowers his eyes and sees a black woman washing clothes, feeling sorry for her fate and pondering about the "enigma of our miserable human destiny."[11] She does not see him and begins singing one of his songs—"Of the sweetness in your eyes / The breeze is envious"—which he welcomes as a consolation.[12] What we see in this episode is a propagation of voices that, previously recorded in print and now vocalized by its readers and listeners, succeed and superpose one another. Ricardo lends his voice to Africa's voice, which Castro Alves had recorded in his poem, only to realize that they—Ricardo and the poet—are actually giving voice to an Afro-Brazilian woman who, in turn, puts one of Ricardo's pieces to her voice. Hearing his voice in another's, Ricardo associates this with yet another doubling of voices: Domingos Caldas Barbosa singing his modinha*s* and *lundus* to Portuguese aristocrats, under the Arcadian name Lereno.[13]

In Lima Barreto's text, Castro Alves's verse serves as a metaphor for an idealized relationship between the speaker/singer's voice and the ear of the Other, which, in "Vozes d'África," is the Supreme Listener. In the poem, God seems to have turned a deaf ear to all of Africa's plight, and the continent, in turn, seeks another ear, one that would completely absorb its lamentation and leave no trace of it: "If I weep . . . the scorching sand drinks my tears; / perhaps . . . so that my lament, oh merciful God! / Thou shall not discover on the land."[14] As a metaphor for sound reception, the image of tears absorbed by sand suggests that listening should operate as a sort of incorporation, through which sound is completely dispersed in the receiving body. Furthermore, it points out that, like the sand, the listening body always consists of a multiplicity of bodies that function as one. One may call this coherence of the listening body "Glory" (to use Ricardo's term). Influenced by the black woman singing his song, as well as the comfort he finds in that, Ricardo sits down to compose a new modinha on the theme of Glory and its fleeting, impalpable nature. It reminds him of breath that cannot be grasped with one's hands or of Love, with its burning powers; hence, he cannot put it down to paper. "The emotion had been strong"— the narrator tells us—"all of his nature had been tilled, jumbled up with the idea of someone stealing his merit away from him. He could not quiet his thoughts, catch the words in the air, feel the music buzzing in his ears."[15] That Ricardo should not be able to record Glory suggests that a synthesis of all voices in a listening body may constitute a Romantic Absolute—always within the horizon of one's desire but still untenable.

Such an absolute cannot obfuscate the fact that one of these voices is silenced—namely, that of the black woman. After the woman finishes singing, Ricardo remarks:

> —You're doing well, Dona Alice, you're doing well! If not, why would I ask you for an *encore*?
> The girl raised her head, realized who was talking and said:
> —I didn't know you were there, Sir, otherwise I wouldn't have sung in your presence.
> —Nonsense! I assure you that it's very, very good. Please, sing.
> —Not on my life! I don't want you to pass no judgment on me. . . .
> Although he insisted several times, the girl refused to continue.[16]

The reason for such a refusal is twofold: the girl is clearly embarrassed for having sung in the presence of the song's composer, but she is also aware of the social differences between the two of them, even though they both live in a poor neighborhood. Ricardo is the one who has access to canonical texts from Luso-Brazilian literature, whereas she mispronounces a word— she says "acriticar" instead of "criticar"—which indicates her lack of formal education. Such a discrepancy between Ricardo's and the black woman's access to cultural products is also apparent in the difference between how Ricardo expects his voice to be heard—as teardrops absorbed by the sand— and how he imagines the black woman's voice to be a touch, a caress. Contrary to what he expects from his listeners, when Ricardo himself listens to the black woman, there is no incorporation but rather a contact between two very distinct, yet empathetic, bodies.

Interspersing these two modes of listening, the authorial voice tends to agglutinate under its name all nonauthorial voices. Rather than compose a polyphonic event, such voices make up a palimpsest, inasmuch as certain voices tend to disappear under the author's name. It is no coincidence that the chapter in which Ricardo hears the black woman sing ends with a girl begging him to send her a copy of his song "Os teus braços" (Your arms), which is yet another metaphor for the amorous-like contact between sound and listener, but one that does not allow for any incorporation. The narrative describes two distinct sonic events: in the voice of an ordinary singer, all voices tend to a polyphonic coexistence; in the voice of an autho-rial singer, a name is reproduced, to which any resonating voice is associ-ated. In between one and the other, there remains a certain anxiety, given the uncertainties of popular music, which always slips outside the fixity of recordings or names.

Nameless Resoundings

In the beginning of the twentieth century, several songs were still linked to communal performances and therefore bear no authorial figure, stricto sensu, but rather draw together a cluster of voices, posing a problem to listeners. Not hearing the authorial voice that sustains an organic whole, listeners are left with a polyphony that has no easily identifiable "origi-nary" producer. Two of the songs that Casa Edison recorded bear such marks: "Isto é bom," composed by Xisto Bahia (1841–1894) and recorded by Eduardo das Neves (1874–1919), and "Bolim bolacho," an anonymous song recorded by Baiano (1887–1944).[17] In both compositions, the refrain functions as a thread that the singer uses to stitch the song together in a rhapsodic form. In "Isto é bom," for example, one might relate all the stan-zas to the refrain "Isto é bom, isto é bom que dói," which literally means "This is good, this is so good that it hurts" (that is, it is extremely good). Nonetheless, the stanzas do not compose a logical narrative sequence. Bearing traces of orally composed songs, they operate, instead, as sepa-rate units that advance certain formulaic thoughts, similar to the Indians' "Carta canta" in Palma's tradición, by means of juxtaposition.[18] Thus, the singer says: "Se eu brigar com meus amores / Não se intrometa ninguém /

Que acabados os arrufos / Ou eu vou, ou ela vem" (If I fight with my lovers / It's no one's business / When the bickering is over / Either I go to her, or she comes to me).[19] Not an individual viewpoint, these verses are also not merely a cliché or commonsensical idea that the composer put to words and music. Rather, a voice resonates, to which the singer's own is incorporated; it is a voice whose traces are hard to pinpoint, even when one can feel its presence the most, as when the black woman's voice caresses Ricardo.[20] Contrasting the easiness of popular music production and consumption with the desire for an absolute in classical music, Machado de Assis's story "Um homem célebre" plays on the tension between nameless sounds and authorial voices.[21]

The tale begins with an interpellation—"Ah! o senhor é que é o Pestana?" (Oh, so you're Pestana?)—indicating that, even though the author's name is known, not everyone is able to associate name to person.[22] Such a gap between name and anonymity allows the composer to witness, as a spectator or listener, the vicissitudes of his songs, once they become public. Heading home after the reunion, at which a young girl (Sinhazinha Mota) interpellated him, Pestana hears sounds coming from inside a house. Someone is playing his latest composition on a clarinet while others dance to the tune, and, right after that, Pestana sees two men walking down the street and hears them whistling the very same song. The composer reaches what the narrator had previously called, referring to one of Pestana's polkas, "a consagração do assobio e da cantarola noturna" (the pinnacle of fame that is the whistling and the nightly singing).[23] Frustrated with his inability to compose anything but danceable polkas—he keenly desires to become a classical-music composer, like Beethoven or Mozart—Pestana dashes home desperately and shuts the door behind him. As if they voice a collective unconscious, the melodies Pestana composes become a public property of sorts, sung simultaneously in so many places, both private and public. As such, they no longer need their author, and Pestana's running away from them enacts not only his anguish as a composer but also the works' detachment from their author. The door shuts, and the composer and his sounds may follow quite different paths; in the long run, the author's name may ultimately be erased from the singers' minds.[24]

Such erasure, the story suggests, is precluded only if Pestana manages to write "just one such immortal page," such as Mozart's or Beethoven's.[25] As if popular music could never bring forth an "immortal," page-bound name, Pestana, in his many efforts to compose "serious works, profound, inspired, and carefully wrought," would invariably end up repeating pieces by immortal names.[26] Ultimately, instead of achieving one such name, Pestana is forced to face "an immense, invisible Pestana," whose listeners—and their mode of listening—the composer had been eschewing all along.[27] Pestana's immensity lies not only in his popularity and the number of listeners singing his songs but also in the impetus with which they assign a function to them in their personal and social lives. His invisibility, on the other hand, reveals that such immensity functions in the author's absence, lacking a name. Invisible to others, Pestana becomes all the more visible to himself, as the self-image that only the Others' voices could compose for him.[28]

That the author's name may subsume to his listeners' singing is suggested when the same girl who initially interpellated Pestana briefly entertains the idea of marrying the composer before falling asleep to the sound of the polka, which she had learned by heart. If, married, Pestana expected from his wife nothing less than the inspiration he could not find as a single man, Sinhazinha Mota's fantasy betrays the desire to link up the author's name and her own, private, familial performances. Against immortal pages, popular music listeners quickly memorize melodies and move away from music scores and engage in other activities while singing, such as falling asleep or walking down the street. Pestana's and his listeners' desires thus take quite opposite courses.

In his fruitless attempts to compose an immortal page, Pestana stands by the window, stargazing: "To him the stars seemed like so many musical notes affixed to the sky, just waiting for somebody to unfasten them. Someday the sky would be emptied, but by then the earth would be a constellation of musical scores."[29] From scattered, simultaneous, disconnected sounds, Pestana wishes to engender a reproducible written structure that might hamper the distance that oral memorization establishes between the song and its author. In Pestana's vision, what the world would lose in terms of a multiplicity of sounds, even though unstructured, it should gain in terms of immortality, all under an author's name. To his listeners, on the contrary, music, learned by heart and sung while performing other activities, retained a degree of unconsciousness and incorporeality that would only be underscored by sound transmission and recording.

Disembodiment and *les Revenants* (Hearing Ghostly Voices Again)

Notorious because it is considered by many to be the first song to be recorded and labeled as a samba, "Pelo telefone" is also a key song within the history of Brazilian popular music due to the polemics around its authorship.[30] Although the song bears authorial names, it is indebted to a communal mode of composition, evinced in its structure and reworking of folkloric motifs and reinforced by the inclusion of sound transmission technology in its lyrics.[31] Comparing "Pelo telefone" to other songs with the same Carnival topos, such as "Iaiá, ioiô" (1930), by Josué de Barros (1888–1959),[32] one sees that the effect the telephone brings about is that of a fuzzy origin. In Barros's song, the masters' presence is clearly felt, even though their voices are not heard, but in Donga's, the interlocutor is not physically present, but his voice has been heard. If it is true that, as Sandroni points out, the *chefe da polícia*—which appeared originally in a newspaper article—turns into the song's *chefe da folia*,[33] one must also note that the historical figure becomes a mythical one and that this shift entails a completely different structure. In the recording of "Iaiá, ioiô," the singer—Carmen Miranda—expresses her desire to enjoy Carnival by explaining to her masters, in a very sensible manner, all the reasons why she should be allowed to go out and celebrate. Carnival is such a good party: three days of sheer happiness, driving people out of their minds. So, if the masters do not wish to go enjoy themselves, they should at least let her do it. In "Pelo telefone," by contrast, the voice the singer hears over the phone does not verbalize an individual's speech but rather the clear command of a desire that, with an uncertain origin, belongs to everyone. Having the force of an unconscious order uttered in the present—the original says, "o chefe da folia / pelo telefone / *manda* me avisar"—that voice can neither be questioned on the level of logical discourse nor be connected to any individual body. It comes from us to ourselves, through the wire, and it diffuses into a feeling of happiness and corporeal skills that contrast with the *rolinha*'s ineptitude.

As Sandroni demonstrates, the stanza about the rolinha is a response to several folkloric verses in which the image of the bird caught in a string functions as a metaphor for those who do not know how to deal with love's many traps.[34] In "Pelo telefone," the poetic voice replies to such an image by stating that the rolinha was caught precisely because it did not know how to do the samba. Therefore, the samba is no longer merely a music or dance form, but one that allows its performers to act effectively in other social situations; true *sambistas* are able to establish erotic ties without being tied emotionally to them. In this sense, the strings and ties that are evoked in the stanza about the rolinha contrast with the wire implicit in the very expression *pelo telefone* (over the phone). Unable to samba, the bird becomes a massive body, caught in its own physicality, incapable of movement, whereas the sambista, through his skillful hearing, accepts the music's impact on his body and thus transforms it into a moving, expanding corporeality that avoids constraining strings. In "Pelo telefone," the body of popular music connects itself to the telephone wire, responding to the phantasmatic voices one may hear through it and counterposing, years in advance, the corporeal constraints inscribed in Noel Rosa's "Rapaz folgado."[35]

What the rolinha's ineptitude and entanglement in bows, strings, and lines suggest is that the constrained body becomes more material in its disregard for the body's excesses and its capacity to hear sounds in movement. Sound recording and transmitting technologies would compensate for that, creating a phantasmatic sonic body. As Evan Eisenberg notes, playing a record is like invoking ghostly voices coming "from another world— something voices are good at"—even though we cannot quite discern where they really come from.[36] In fact, the record listener and the musician are "like a man and his familiar ghost," for they "do not inhabit the same world."[37] This difference is "the premise of their intimacy. And their intimacy is only closer when the ghost is heard but not seen, since it then seems that the two worlds are not tangential, but coextensive."[38] Technology, in this respect, only enhanced what was already potentially there in the nature of sound, in its capacity to be carried away from its point of origin, as Raimundo Correia's poem "As pombas" suggests.

When Ricardo, in Lima Barreto's novel, alludes to the Parnassian poem, he uses it as a positive comparison to his songs' popularity—both are out there, skipping from mouth to mouth, ear to ear. Correia's poem contrasts pigeons with dreams; whereas the first fly out of the dovecote at daybreak and return at dusk, the latter also fly out of our hearts once we become adolescents, but they never come back.[39] In this sense, the pigeons function as a symbol for the songs' trajectories—from the singer's mouth to the listeners' ears, looping back to the former once listeners learn them by heart and reproduce them. If we take into account the dreams, however, the poem as a metaphor renders sonic exchanges more complex, articulating the notion of return and loss, loyalty and betrayal. Thus, although it seems accurate to perceive record listening as a spectral event, it is no less true that such ghostly voices also bring about a nostalgia for a certain presence, as we may hear in "Triste jandaia" (Sad jandaia), another composition by Josué de Barros and one of the first songs Carmen Miranda recorded.[40]

A *canção-toada* in a rather melancholic tone, the song expresses a longing for rural life. Such longing is underscored by the fact that the song revolves around an absence, a loss. In the song, a countrywoman is troubled because she cannot find her *jandaia,* a parakeet common in Brazil. A beautiful and sweet bird, the jandaia is saddened by the fact that the rooster sings, but she herself is unable to and is always sobbing, joyless. Preoccupied, the singer asks another parakeet about the jandaia's whereabouts, ordering that it seek her in the corn fields without eating any of the corn, which is for the rooster's lunch. In this contrast between the rooster and the jandaia—the singer and the one devoid of musicality, respectively—it should be noted that the jandaia hides exactly in the fields that grow food for the rooster. If one displaces this image metaphorically in order to include the rooster's main attribute in the song—that it is capable of singing—one might say that it gets its food for singing from the same fields where the jandaia finds a hiding place. If the rooster sings—almost professionally, since one of its main tasks is to announce the break of day and the beginning of our daily tasks—it is because those anonymous, hidden voices provide it with the sounds, even if unmusical, for it to sing. Its singing is born out of a sonic collectivity: the corn fields. That the countrywoman should miss the jandaia is thus understandable. Even if, to a certain extent, she privileges the rooster, she cannot live without the jandaia's presence, even sonically speaking. Uncertain as to whether the parakeet will be able to bring the jandaia back or not, the singer must concentrate on yet another predicament: a hawk is attacking her chicks and eating the corn. Coming from up high, the hawk might leave the countrywoman without the jandaia or the rooster, devouring both musical, individual singing and unmusical, collective sounds. In this relational system the song describes, the singer risks losing it all.

Such potential loss is counterbalanced by the fact that popular songs are cultural artifacts that pay special attention to generational linkage and the altered continuity of time in tradition. Ghostly voices do return then, even if they are not quite the same. One may hear such voices in "Pequinês e pitbull" (Pekingese and pit bull), a samba by Gabriel Moura, Lulu Aranha, and Jovi Joviniano, and which Seu Jorge recorded for the album released in Brazil as *Samba esporte fino* (2001).[41] In the song, the singer complains that he does not want to leave his home to go to the bar and shoot some pool. Too many people are bugging him, but he is not going out. The song begins with a linear narrative, such as the ones composers would create as authors with pencil and paper in hand. However, once this narrative is sung twice, the song breaks up into short sayings, following the one with which the singer closes the first narrative: "o que não falta é tatu, pra me levar pro buraco" (there are plenty of armadillos, trying to take me down the hole). Of these sayings, two are sung partly with a female chorus: "a parrot that follows a *joão-de-barro* / gets in trouble / and ends up as a bricklayer's assistant" and "a Pekingese that wants to fight a pit bull / is out of its mind / and ends up as vultures' picnic."[42] Initially, the singer identifies the women in the chorus as "minhas meninas" (my girls), but later he clarifies that they are members of the *Velha Guarda da Mangueira*—that is, the oldest members in one of the first schools of samba in Rio de Janeiro. That these voices should be heard separately from that of the singer certainly constitutes a tribute to those women who symbolize the matriarchs of samba—women who, like Tia Ciata, were responsible for the social milieu that engendered the samba as a musical form. Such an homage occurs precisely when the song's narration breaks up, and therefore the formulaic sayings that resemble the old rhapsodic mode of singing and composing—as in "Pelo telefone"—coincide with the recovery of those collective voices that are often forgotten in favor of the author or singer.

Within the context of the oral performance of "Pequinês e pitbull," one might suggest that the sayings in the song formulate a possible reply to the dilemma that the jandaia faces in Barros's song as well as to the singer's longing and imminent loss. If the jandaia is torn between desiring to sing and not being able to, the women's collective voices in "Pequinês e pitbull" might have something to tell with their sayings: one should not try to be or behave like someone else. The parrot's, the Pekingese's, and the jandaia's troubles all stem from that error. Even though such ethical resolution might sound somewhat simplistic, one should not overlook its power when it comes to safeguarding a space for the existence of ghostly voices. Seu Jorge's oral quote from one of Mestre Marçal's sayings underscores this point: "You may fill up the swimming pool, but don't empty my wash basin." Given an unequal distribution of and access to cultural resources and production—such as the hawk's attacks in Barros's song—it is imperative that a social space be kept, wherein collective voices, such as the jandaia's in the corn fields, may speak and be heard. Eventually, authorial singers, such as Seu Jorge, recover these voices and often name them. Even if they are merely traces of a presence—a name with no voice, which leaves a brief impression, or an uncomprehended listener who tends to disappear—or traces that remain within their own spaces of recognition, alongside the disembodiment that sound transmission and recording affect, they are recovered under other voices and forge new polyphonies. Certain voices may be forever lost, such as Tia Ciata's or that of Dona Alice, the black woman who silences before Ricardo, the modinha singer in Lima Barreto's novel. In their disappearance, though, they call for the recording of other voices such as theirs and for a listening practice that will allow us to hear—as I attempted to point out in this chapter—certain issues surrounding their recording: the inevitable superposition of voices, the friction between a name and nameless resoundings, and the never complete disembodiment that technology affords us.

2

RADIO TRANSVESTISM AND THE GENDERED
SOUNDSCAPE IN BUENOS AIRES, 1930s–1940s

Christine Ehrick

IN EARLY 1932, a small item appeared in Argentina's first popular radio magazine *Antena*. Carrying the headline "A woman singing what is meant for a man is ugly, but a man acting like a little woman is intolerable," the article was the opening shot in a campaign against what we might call transgendered performance on the Argentine airwaves.[1] This item is also a departure point for an exploration of debates and struggles over gender and vocality during the golden age of Argentine broadcasting. By breaching the boundaries of public and private and separating the voice from any immediate visual referent, radio technology itself was anxiety-provoking. Radio also intersected with the ongoing disruptions of traditional hierarchies of class, gender, and citizenship that characterized the era, amplifying and diffusing anxieties generated by these disruptions across a wide spectrum of society. In 1930s and 1940s Argentina, in other words, radio was a key forum within which shifting constructions of class, citizenship, gender and sexuality merged with the fantasies and fears provoked by technological modernization.

In her book *Vested Interests: Cross Dressing and Cultural Anxiety,* Marjorie Garber writes of the transvestite effect, which she defines as "the overdetermined appearance of the transvestite" at moments of new and significant challenges to the existing social and cultural order: "The transvestite . . . is both terrifying and seductive precisely because s/he incarnates and emblematizes the disruptive element that intervenes, signaling not just another category crisis, but—much more disquietingly—a crisis of 'category' itself."[2] In the golden age radio press of Buenos Aires, Argentina (and to a lesser extent Montevideo, Uruguay), one finds evidence to support Garber's ideas. Here, the appearance of the radio transvestite (real or imagined) personified a broader "category crisis" in politics and society in the region. Worries that feminism was creating a new generation of man-hating *marimachos,* for example, coupled with neurasthenic suspicions that modern urban society was making men soft and perhaps even less heterosexual, intersected with the fantasy and anxiety evoked by the mystery of the radio receiver.[3] Argentine political discourse at the time was also replete with suspicions about the pernicious influence of "foreigners"—immigrants, Jews, and others defined as outsiders—who were associated with and accused of gender and other subversions. Modernity, in other words, carried with it a number of overlapping threats to the Argentine national family.

We often understand transvestism as being synonymous with cross-dressing and visual constructions of gender. Yet, if we define transvestism as "a performance of gender" that complicates and subverts traditional binary notions of masculine and feminine, that performance can be vocal as well as visual.[4] The (adult) human voice is immediately and deeply gendered; in the case of radio, voice becomes a primary way in which gender is communicated. In different ways and with different connotations, 1930s Argentine radio featured women vocalizing like men and men vocalizing like women. Though we might more properly classify some of these performances in terms of androgyny rather than transvestism, the fact that critics classified them in terms of the latter helps to situate gender-bending radio/sound performances within the broader context of Argentine politics and related gender discourses.

The radio/aural transvestite could assume many forms: a man singing "women's songs," a woman who dared to adopt male oratory style, and a suspiciously androgynous female singer, among others. In this sense, radio transvestism has commonalities with blackface performance, a term that connotes the visual but which has always had strong vocal dimensions as well.[5] In the same way that transvestism is a performance of gender, blackface is a performance of race. By separating the body's aural and visual components, radio greatly facilitated such vocal sleight of hand. Despite these similarities, blackface performance did more to reinforce than subvert racial hierarchies and stereotypes, whereas transvestite/drag performances could be more slippery. As Matthew Murray argues, while so-called lavender gentleman radio performances in the United States ultimately reinforced homophobia and heteronormativity, radio transvestism could in some cases disrupt and complicate traditional gender constructions.[6] In Argentina, these types of performances were met with campaigns aimed at asserting vocal heteronormativity as part of a larger campaign to "professionalize" Argentine broadcasting during the 1930s.

This chapter explores ways in which radio voices performed gender, especially moments when those voices challenged and subverted the gendered order and disrupted the gendered soundscape via the introduction of unorthodox pairings of voice and speech or voice and seen body. Radio's capacity to elasticize identity construction is grounded in the fact that sound emanating from a radio receiver is never "synched" with any image. Moreover, the intimacy and immediacy of the human voice invites listeners to come up with their own imagery (in the "mind's eye") to suit the sounds and voices they are hearing. Radio is thus invocatory of the cultural imaginary in ways, perhaps, that visual media are not—stimulating that cultural imaginary in ways that evoked both fantasy and fear. Radio transvestism existed both as an example of the medium's capacity to transcend traditional boundaries of space and culture and as a straw man for those seeking to reimpose those boundaries.

Radio, Bodies, and the Gendered Soundscape

Many sound scholars employ the concept of the soundscape as a way of emphasizing the historically and culturally constructed aspects of sound and the perception of sound. A soundscape, in Emily Thompson's words, is an "auditory or aural landscape" and a way of emphasizing the sonic dimensions of our constructed environment.[7] Scholars have paid less attention to the gendered dimensions of the soundscape. In *Gender and Qualitative Methods*, Helmi Järviluoma, Pirkko Moisala, and Anni Vilkko introduce the term *gendered soundscape*, asking readers to contemplate the way gender—and gendered hierarchies—may be projected and heard in sound environments. We "learn gender through the total sensorium," as they put it, and gender is also represented, contested, and reinforced through the aural.[8] Of the ways in which gender is reinforced, challenged, or renegotiated through the aural, the human voice is by far the most obvious conveyance. The soundscape echoes prevailing social hierarchies, with certain dominant voices claiming authority and rationality, while other voices remain muted or are dismissed as mere "noise."[9] Historically speaking, male voices have been associated with the former category, whereas female and other voices deemed inferior or less rational have been relegated to the latter. In other words, by listening to the soundscape—especially its vocal components—one can perceive sonic dimensions of patriarchy and challenges to that patriarchal order.

When contemplating the gendered soundscape, we unavoidably bump into another important, complex component of gender and sound: the relationship between voice and body. Although a full discussion of this issue lies beyond the scope of this chapter, it is important to pause briefly to interrogate the prevailing tendency to refer to radio voices (as well as voice-off and voice-over in film) as *disembodied*.[10] On its most basic level, the notion of disembodiment does not do justice to the complexities, texture, and physicality of the human voice. It also minimizes how much we rely on the voice and vocal performance as a signifier, listening for socially and historically constructed cues as to the speaker's gender, class, ethnicity, age, and sexual identity. Like other aspects of gender, voice differences have biological roots, but gendered constructions of the human voice vary widely over time and place.[11] Rather than *disembodied*, film scholar Michel Chion uses the term *acousmatic* to describe voices or other sounds with sources that are not readily seen or discernible. The term carries the negative of adding more jargon to an already overcrowded palette, but it allows for a more unfettered exploration of the voice/body relationship.[12] Radio vocalizations, I argue, represent a projection and performance of the body, which in turn highlight the fact that the voice is a critical way in which the body performs gender, class, and ethnicity.[13]

Asserting that vocalizations are in some way embodied does not mean that relationships between voice and other elements of the body are in any way fixed. Just as the seen body can be transgendered, so can the heard body. What if a feminine voice was emanating from a biologically male body—or a body suspected of being biologically male? What if the voice of a female singer crossed into what is generally considered a male register? What if a masculine voice was performing with lyrics meant for a woman? What if a female voice was speaking in an authoritative style—commentary or oratory—historically associated with a male voice? Even more pronounced than a dislike of women adopting "male" oratory style on radio were fears that radio was providing a cover for trangendered males, seducing listeners with their femininity, evoking homoerotic desire on the part of male listeners, and generally blurring the boundaries of vocal heteronormativity. The relationship of the human voice to the body, in other words, is highly unstable and far more complex than the notion of *disembodiment* implies. Radio rendered it more so, with its interactive process wherein as listeners we "conjure up a body we don't get to see," cultivating both fantasy and anxiety among the audience.[14]

Twentieth-century modernity brought new challenges to traditional gender roles and constructions, and it spurred fears that these changes threatened the very fabric of home, family, and nation. In belle epoque Argentina, the influx of (mostly male) European immigrants and the radical political ideas they brought with them generated a great deal of anxiety among medical and political reformers who saw sexual subversion as one of many threats to Argentine culture.[15] Radio appears to have reignited, redirected, and diffused these anxieties. In this chapter, I focus on three events in which radio/aural transvestism made an appearance: the 1932 campaign of radio magazine *Antena* against transgendered radio performance, the rise and fall of scandal surrounding Mexican contralto Elvira Ríos in 1943–1944, and rightist/nationalist radio discourse and corresponding radio legislation during the 1940s. My larger interest is in examining the intersections of these trajectories and in understanding the ways radio both reflected and helped to define the debates and struggles over gender and gender identity in the first half of the twentieth century.

Antena's 1932 Campaign Against "Sonic Drag"

In early 1932, a series of editorials in Argentina's first popular radio magazine *Antena* took on the issue of "immoral" and "ridiculous" radio performances, which are perhaps best described as radio transvestism. The first editorial—mentioned previously and entitled "A woman singing what is meant for a man is ugly, but a man acting like a little woman is intolerable"—acknowledged a history of such performance on the stage, but it made a distinction between theater, in which, the author argues, certain kinds of impersonations might be acceptable (if not always welcome) and radio, for which more realism was required. There is, of course, a long history of gender impersonation on stage, but, in most cases, the audience was supposed to know that a woman was playing a male role, or vice versa.[16] Transgender stage performances, in other words, were often nonacousmatic, and they did not reach their audiences on the sly.

In this transition from stage to radio, the acousmatic nature of radio heightened the possibility for deception.[17] To make its point, the article painted a visual picture for the reader/listener, a picture which may or may not have had anything to do with reality. "Let us imagine a young man, tall and strong, weeping because 'her' boyfriend has abandoned her, the poor innocent, after having deceived her and promised his eternal love. . . . Let us imagine a fifty-something, balding and pot-bellied citizen, lamenting his fate as an offended 'girl,' hysterical about some recent disappointment she had suffered." Society should, the piece concluded, "prevent at all costs that men cease to be men, even in front of the microphone." Radio stations must insist and ensure, the piece continued, that performers are assigned a place "corresponding to their sex," and that "men sing songs meant for them and not resort to lyrics that are 'eminently feminine.'"[18] A second article reinforced the idea that on radio there should be no room for gender bending. "Men must not only differentiate themselves from women by their clothing. This difference must always be expressed, and strongly so, in their spirit and way of being and acting."[19] In other words, clear gender distinctions—especially on the radio—must be expressed in aural and visual ways.

The series also differentiated between female and male gender masquerade, not surprisingly expressing greater anxiety for the latter. "Isn't it more than ridiculous that a girl, sometimes in her forties, takes the microphone and sings a song meant for a man—and a real man at that? A woman must always be a woman. . . . But the man who enthusiastically takes on a song written for women? This is not merely ridiculous. It is low-class and even immoral."[20] The follow-up article went a step further, questioning both the masculinity and the sexuality of men singing "women's songs." "The repertoire of songs for men is inexhaustible," it stated, "so much so that if certain singers resort to effeminacy, we suspect that this must be due to an invincible inclination, and not because circumstances require it."[21] This piece turned up the heat markedly, and the picture painted here is not

simply one of odd or pathetic behavior; rather, it is one of deliberately immoral acts by men who are identified—indirectly but clearly, it seems—as
homosexuals. Finally, the anonymous radio critic invoked the power of the
market and popular taste to encourage stations to ban such performances
from the airwaves, arguing that they were out of step with listener tastes
and provoked the "disgust" of the audience. Radio, in other words, was out
of synch with the cultural norms of Argentines, and in this they were putting their economic futures at risk. Those male performers who persist in
"cultivating effeminacy," the article concluded, should be dropped from
the station, or the listener will drop the station himself or herself. Such
performances, moreover, could have wider implications as the day may
arrive when a "real" man would never set foot in a radio station.[22] Radio,
in this scenario, risked becoming something of a ghetto of the vulgar, an
electronic cabaret permanently alienated from the "respectable" classes of
Argentina.

As historians, we have no referent here; we do not know anything
about what these performances really consisted of, how common they
were, if there was a particular station or stations where these performances
were concentrated, and so on. Even though we do not know the answers
to these questions, it is helpful here to entertain the possibility that these
were tango performances. Sylvia Molloy, for example, has written about
tango and its "tendency towards transvestism, to a provocative and stimulating sexual confusion."[23] Female tango singers of the 1920s and 1930s,
most notably Azucena Maizani, were known to don men's clothing and
sing songs written for males.[24] Not surprisingly, there was more toler-
ance for female cross-dressing than for male. Regardless of whether the
performances targeted in *Antena* were tango performances, the critiques
seem to come from a similar place: concerns that previously stage-based
performances with origins in the cabaret tradition and which tended toward greater or lesser degrees of gender ambiguity were making their way
onto the airwaves. This remediation, which had the effect of making these
performances both acousmatic and consumable by the general public, significantly upped the ante.

One month after the first articles appeared, *Antena* announced tri-
umphantly that several radio stations had declared they would no longer
permit men to perform songs written for women over the airwaves. *Antena* presented this move as the beginning of a much-needed "prophylactic
work" on radio, one of the goals of which was that "the definition of the

sexes be energetically enforced."[25] This phrase merits a pause, because it is such a clear articulation of the perception that radio carried the potential to threaten vocal heteronormativity, and the pressing need within some quarters to ensure that radio reinforce, rather than subvert, traditional gender distinctions and norms.

This specific campaign dovetailed with others going on in Argentina, inside and outside the boundaries of broadcasting. The campaign against men singing women's songs was closely followed, for example, by a campaign in the radio press against women commentators, orators, and poetry recitationists. During the early 1930s, there was room for an eclectic range of female voices on Buenos Aires radio. However, starting in late 1933 and into 1934, a flurry of commentary in the radio press questioned women's qualifications to speak and recite poetry on the airwaves. As elsewhere, women speakers on Argentine radio were criticized as annoying and hard on the ears.[26] Female speakers were also mocked for their attempts to speak *"en cátedra,"* a term which refers to the authoritative speech of the priest or the professor. The lack of innate female ability to speak with authority and personality turned such radio performances into a pathetic mockery, and they were an example of amateurism and "vulgarity" on the radio.[27] The sequestering of female voices—out of the "male" sphere of commentary and into the proper arenas of domestic advice, chat, children's programs, and singing—was also presented as part of radio's professionalization.[28] I suggest that we understand campaigns against men singing women's songs and the mockery of female orators as two sides of the same coin. The campaign against women commentators echoed the same call for radio to "energetically enforce" the definition of the sexes. Male voices performing "women's songs" and female voices speaking "en cátedra," both of which critics singled out as examples of "vulgarity" on the airwaves, can both be read as examples of "aural transvestism" that destabilized the gendered soundscape and threatened radio's reputation.

The *Antena* campaign also coincided with the beginning of a new— and in some ways unprecedented—repression of gay men in Argentina. Between mid-1932 and late 1933, a series of new laws expanded the circumstances under which police could detain and imprison men accused of homosexuality, laws which shut down many gay bars and made it illegal for a suspected homosexual to even be seen with a minor in public.[29] As the decade progressed, this discourse about the need for prophylactic work to "professionalize" the airwaves merged with an increasingly vocal nationalist, Catholic, anti-Semitic, and homophobic Right, which tended to associate popular radio not only with "vulgarity" but also with corrupting foreign elements that were associated with the United States and with Jews especially.[30] By this point, *radioteatro* (or radio dramas) had emerged as an important element in daytime and prime-time radio, and it became the new focus for conservative radio critics. Here, it was not just the content but also the sound of radio drama that made the medium so harmful. In June 1934, the official Catholic newspaper *El Pueblo* attacked a particular radio drama for presenting "a voice with unfriendly affectation, an unctuous cadence and an aftertaste of the slums," which provoked mental illness in young and older women alike.[31] Another *El Pueblo* article later that month called for stronger regulation of radio speech, asserting that the only people allowed on the air should be those "who are morally, intellectually and physically healthy, and who by the precision and clarity of their speech, honesty of expression and tone of voice, show themselves to be normal, complete, and capable men, worthy of speaking to the invisible world who is listening."[32] This excerpt approaches the language used by *Antena* in 1932, although the definition of what was meant by "normal, complete, and capable men" is not made clear. These articles are also significant in that they are calling on outside (that is, state) intervention to ensure that only "real men" speak on the air.

Elvira Ríos: Seduction and Suspicion

Although the clamor over vocal cross-dressing on the radio seems to have subsided after the *Antena* campaign of 1932, anxieties over male performers sounding like or posing as women, it seems, did not entirely disappear. One must skip ahead another decade to find the next evidence of such fears of gender deception in the curious case of Mexican singer Elvira Ríos. Ríos (1914–1987) was an important singer in Mexico, primarily known for her interpretations of the boleros of Mexican composer Agustín Lara. Ríos, therefore, was in some cases performing songs originally written for men. More important, however, was Ríos's singing voice: a velvety contralto that occupied a somewhat ambiguous place on the vocal scale. As a genre, bolero itself went against the grain of vocal heteronormativity. "The bolero is the music of the androgynous voice," writes La Fountain-Stokes, "deep in the case of women; ethereal, almost falsetto, when performed by men . . .

a music of indeterminate love objects, of ambiguity, of the you and the me, in spite of your sex, or precisely because of your unnamable sex."[33]

All of this, coupled no doubt with Ríos's foreignness, gave shape to a short-lived but historically significant rumor about the singer's gender identity. Argentine radio scholar Carlos Ulanovsky described the incident this way: "On the person of Elvira Ríos fell a weighty suspicion: perhaps because of her deep voice it was rumored that she was a man disguised as a woman."[34] Although there is no evidence to suggest that these were anything but rumors, by placing this incident alongside the earlier campaign described above, we gain insight into the ways in which modern sound media—phonographs but especially radio—were intersecting with broader anxieties that modernity was undermining traditional gender roles and boundaries, and in the process creating openings for "vulgar" and "immoral" elements to infiltrate the homes and ears of upstanding citizens under cover of invisibility.

Elvira Ríos arrived in Buenos Aires in March 1942 with an exclusive broadcast contract with Radio El Mundo and a contract to make at least one film with an Argentine studio. Critics lauded her radio debut, and rumors circulated about a love affair between Ríos and Orson Welles, who was visiting Buenos Aires at the time. When Ríos departed for Brazil somewhat hastily a few months later, it was rumored that she was meeting up with Welles.[35] It was during this time in Brazil that a series of rumors began to circulate about the singer, first in Brazil itself, it seems, and then moving south to Uruguay and then to Argentina. Along with rumors of espionage and drugs were those suggesting Ríos was engaged in some kind of gender masquerade.

In July 1943, the Uruguayan publication *Cine Radio Actualidad* presented this matter with no subtlety. The magazine ran a two-page spread with the headline "Is Elvira Ríos a man?" Questions about Ríos's biological sex emerged, it was explained, with an alleged automobile accident in Argentina, after which a medical exam revealed the "truth" about the singer. The singer then soon disappeared and supposedly went to Brazil. Accompanying the article was a large, full-body photograph of Ríos, next to which the magazine posed the question "Are these features masculinely feminine or femininely masculine?" Captioning and arrows around the photo of Ríos's body aid the reader in this dissection, noting, for example, the singer's "broad shoulders," "thin legs," and "somewhat large feet."

More reason for suspicion came from the singer's "exotic and strange voice," and "[it is] with this voice, a mixture of sweetness and deep and passionate tones, that Elvira Ríos has driven half the men of the continent crazy." Herein, it seems, lay the heart of the matter: fears that Ríos, really a biological male, had seduced and excited the passions of male fans, evoking homoerotic desire in Latin American men. "If the story is true," the article continued, "it would be one of the greatest frauds in history."[36] The sensational claims made in this story were quietly and rather half-heartedly retracted in the following issue of *Cine Radio Actualidad*.[37]

A few months later, in September 1943, the Argentine radio publication *Radiolandia* announced, somewhat reluctantly, the need to address the rumors that continued to swirl around the singer. This and another article published six months later speak of the fact that the singer had arrived in Buenos Aires with a contract to perform on Radio El Mundo and to make at least one film with Lumitón studios. Some kind of dispute appears to have emerged, and the singer left Argentina for Brazil with "several months" to go on her radio contract (and perhaps another film obligation). The rumors that she was a man seem to have begun at that point. A later *Radiolandia* article referred to the singer's departure for Brazil and to the "mean-spirited" rumors that had been circulating about her ever since. *Radiolandia* attributed the rumors about Ríos to jealousy and resentment in response to her great success in Buenos Aires. "But one day Elvira went to Brazil," the article explained, to fulfill commitments with a radio station there and to make her second film. At this point, the rumor emerged, source unknown: "Elvira Ríos is a man . . . the police have proven it."[38] *Radiolandia*, for its part, was unequivocal: "Elvira Ríos is a woman and very feminine. The music of her voice speaks, moreover, to her passionate temperament."[39]

Radiolandia called the rumors absurd, especially given that the singer was a mother. Additional rumors claimed that Ríos was a Russian spy and a drug addict and that she had been kicked out of Argentina. *Antena* remained more circumspect. In a September 1943 article, the publication denounced rumors about espionage and drugs but only alluded in the most euphemistic ways to those about her biological sex. "Elvira Ríos: Not a Spy, a Drug Addict, a Russian, nor the Other," read the headline.[40] The timing of this scandal (regardless of its veracity) may be significant. Since we know nothing about the source of these rumors—only that they existed—it is difficult to make any clear attributions. In Argentina, the military coup of June 1943 brought nationalistic, right-wing armed forces into power, which paved the way for the rise of Juan Perón to the presidency three years later. As we will see, both regimes were intensely interested both in language and gender/sexual identity, and they played directly to nationalistic and xenophobic sentiments within the populace.[41]

Argentine Radio Regulations during the 1930s and 1940s: Constructing Flood Walls

Taken together, the *Antena* campaign against radio transvestism and the rumors circulating about Elvira Ríos coincided with two important moments of both regulation of radio speech and repression of male homosexuality in Argentina. In other words, these "appearances" of the radio transvestite arguably occurred at two moments of "category crisis," which, in the Argentine case, both reflected and fueled the expansion of nationalist authoritarianism in Argentina. In asserting new restrictions on both homosexuality and radio performance during the 1930s and 1940s, Argentina was by no means alone. However, by explicitly juxtaposing these trajectories, I underscore the links between these aspects of Argentine nationalist ideology, which in turn helps us to better contextualize the appearances of the radio transvestite in the popular radio press. I would argue that the synchronization of these moves to repress male homosexuality and regulate radio is not coincidental. By linking this history to that of Argentine radio, we see that this homophobic campaign had a sonic dimension as well. The imposition of strict heteronormativity was a cornerstone of Argentine nationalist thought during this era, and the imposition of vocal heteronormativity on the radio was a crucial part of that process.

In 1942 and 1943, a scandal and subsequent trial involving army cadets accused of engaging in all-male "sexual parties" was both a huge embarrassment to the Argentine armed forces and, for right-wing nationalists, clear evidence that the enemy was at the gates. The incident was an underlying factor in the coup of June 1943 that brought members of the fascist-inspired United Officers' Group (GOU) to power, among them a young officer named Juan Perón. Peronism and the military regime preceding it had a strong homophobic current, seeking among other things to reopen bordellos (closed in 1936) as a means of shoring up Argentine male heterosexuality.[42]

The seeds that were planted during the 1930s bore fruit a decade later when the campaign of the Church and Catholic nationalists to purify both the content and language of radio was picked up by sectors of the military regime that seized power in 1943. Composed primarily of rightist nationalist forces within the army and in alliance with Catholic conservatives, the regime imposed new regulations and restrictions on radio, this time with a much more ambitious agenda. In particular, the regime sought to eliminate the use of slang and bad grammar, which was thought to set a bad example for the Argentine population. Shortly after the coup, the *Consejo Superior de Transmisiones Radiotelefónicas* issued a list of words and phrases no longer allowed over the radio.[43] The Argentine state may have gone beyond many others in its attempt to micromanage the use of language over the airwaves. In the campaign to purge U.S. radio comedy of its "lavender gentlemen" and "loose women" during this same era, Matthew Murray notes that in the United States there were "no official rules against male characters having high-pitched voices," and he cites the inability of censors "to control vocal inflections at the time of the performance."[44] The Argentine state, it seems, did attempt to address these issues, seeking to regulate the tone, pitch, or emotion of the radio voice, including some of its transgendered inflections.

One particularly interesting document in this regard is Pedro De Paoli's *Función social de la radiotelefonía,* published in 1943 as a summary of the findings of a government commission on the state of Argentine broadcasting and a platform of suggested reforms and remedies. The book's main conclusion is that "Radio is currently a vehicle of anti-culture. Making it into a strong instrument of culture is the duty of those designated by the State for this mission, and of those who, due to their abilities and patriotism, are in a position to exert their influence in this direction."[45] De Paoli was a pro-Peronist intellectual and an Argentine nationalist in the most xenophobic (racist and anti-Semitic) sense of the term. Time and time again, for example, the moral decay of Argentine radio was laid at the feet of three leading Jewish media figures in Argentina at the time: Radio Belgrano owner Jaime Yankelevich, magazine publisher Julio Korn, and movie mogul Max Glucksmann.[46]

Although it does not explicitly address the issue of transgendered vocalizations, De Paoli's report devotes a great deal of attention to language and voice on the radio. Indeed, according to critics such as De Paoli (and echoing the Catholic critiques of a decade earlier), it was the sonic (and especially vocal) excesses of the radioteatro that were as much, if not more, damaging than the story itself. The tawdry melodrama of radio soaps was especially manifested in their use of sound. These productions are presented as too loud and emotional, but in this description largely within confines of traditional gendered roles. De Paoli, for example, highlights the sadistic nature of the genre by juxtaposing pitiful female sobbing with evil male laughter. "The scenes are infantile and monotonous," he writes. "The little lady cries, cries incessantly, twenty-five minutes of a thirty minute episode; when she speaks she does so in a breathy, weak voice, almost in a whisper . . . while in the meantime the bad man, ruthless and threatening, laughs sarcastically, in a hurtful and mean way, offending the spirit of anyone listening." At the same time, the hero seduces women with his "unctuous voice," which "seems as if it passes over the face and leaves a gelatinous trail."[47] It is worth noting that this phrase—"*la voz pegajosa*" (which roughly translates as an "unctuous" or sticky voice)—was used by both the Catholic press and De Paoli to pejoratively describe the voice of the radio gallant. Female listeners were manipulated by this "gruel," and all of this provoked, in De Paoli's view, something of a crisis of nervous hysteria in the female listener. Women who listened to these dramas, he explained, were often more wrapped up in the characters' problems than in those of their own family. These cheap radio melodramas, in other words, were invading the sanctity of the private home with manipulative stories and sounds, damaging the delicate sensibilities of women. These programs thus undermined women's abilities to be good wives and mothers and weakened the Argentine nation.

After Juan Perón was elected president in February 1946, the new regime wasted little time in implementing changes in radio. As a somewhat nebulous authoritarian ideology, Peronism sought to minimize confusion and ambiguity, creating a world of heroes and villains, oligarchs and "the people," Peronists (patriots) and traitors (anti-Peronists).[48] Peronism did seek an incorporation of women into politics and public life, but it was quite interested in reestablishing clear lines between the sexes: Juan and Eva became the model man and woman, respectively (although Eva embodied a world of contradictions). Peronism, in other words, had no room for mannish women or effeminate men or for excessive vocal emotional outbursts that were not the creation, or under the direction, of the state.

Even before Perón was inaugurated in June 1946, new rules for radio broadcasting were issued. The *Manual de Instrucciones para las Estaciones de Radiodifusión*, published in May 1946, was a lengthy document that addressed and sought to regulate just about every imaginable aspect of radio broadcasting.[49] The Argentine state, under the auspices of its newly created *Dirección General de Radiodifusión,* was now the "moral guardian" of the airwaves. In addition to controlling the kinds of programs that would be on the air (limiting the number of radioteatros that could be broadcast, regulations about how much spoken programming and recorded music was allowed), the new guidelines issued very detailed rules controlling the use of language on the airwaves. The state sought, on one hand, to limit any kind of impromptu speech—including making predictions about the weather—that might deviate from or go beyond official bulletins. On the other hand, the *Manual* also endeavored to restrict the way people spoke on the radio, seeking to eliminate certain "deformations" of the language. Building upon the 1943 regulations on slang and bad grammar, the 1946 regulations sought to rid radio, especially radioteatro, of some of its "melo-dramatic overflow" (yelling, sobbing, moaning, and so on). It is interest-ing to note the gendered aspects of these regulations as well. "The tone of voice," it notes, "including emotional outbursts of the characters, should be what the circumstances demand, but they should always avoid low class falsettos, excessively high-pitched tones, effeminate distortions, etc."[50]

The *Manual* is consistent with the earlier De Paoli document in that it seeks to curb the vocal emotional excesses. In this case, however, trans-gendered vocalizations are more explicitly targeted. The term *falsetto* is one that is mostly associated with male voices. Coupled with the more obvious "effeminate distortions," it seems that the targets of this particu-lar piece of the manual were certain types of "feminine" vocalizations by males. Though it was not a main focus of the efforts of nationalists seek-ing to control the airwaves, the language of the 1946 *Manual* suggests that concerns about vocal cross-dressing on the radio had not entirely dis-appeared. The scope and tone of the critiques also suggest that such per-formances were popular among radio audiences. As elsewhere, it seems, anxieties about radio's boundary blurring were in part a reaction to the fact that so many found pleasure in radio's transgressive qualities. Radio could be evocative of desire and fantasy, and this kind of appeal is precisely what made it dangerous.[51]

Radio in the 1930s and 1940s both reflected and amplified existing anxieties about changing gender roles in Argentine society. Transgendered performances that might have been viewed as crass but acceptable onstage were deemed immoral and offensive when broadcast over the public airwaves and into the private home, without the benefit of a visual referent to provide the audience with clues as to the "true" sex of the performer. The immediacy, intimacy, and sensuality of the human voice made radio transvestism more dangerous than, say, theatrical cross-dressing performances or the literary pen name. In many ways, early radio carried the potential to introduce new fluidity and pluralism into the gendered soundscape and to rework gender identities (at least on the edges) along the way.[52] For a short time, it seems, radio was a place where women could assume "masculine" roles as commentators and announcers and where men could vocally pose as women. Nevertheless, all of this could not last as radio's mass audience expanded.

If radio had the capacity to overflow boundaries of space and culture, the campaigns and regulations can be read as attempts to construct new flood walls to prevent or at least minimize such overflow. Controlling radio speech is ultimately about controlling bodies, including the performance of gender in the public sphere. By seeking to reinforce vocal heteronormativity and curb "feminine excesses" on the airwaves, the Argentine state was in some ways attempting to reassert control over the gendered soundscape and to curb the "flooding out" and boundary blurring that often accompanied it.[53] Peronism certainly did not shy away from melodramatic excess (with its quasireligious cult of adulation toward both Juan and Eva Perón), but those excesses had to be carefully managed and directed and not discharged in directions that might not serve the purposes of the regime.

Pursuing this line of historical research brings us up against an almost inescapable dilemma—that of writing about the sound quality of voices that we cannot and never will hear. We argue for the embodiment of the radio voice when it is precisely the bodily quality of those broadcasts that have not survived (or, in many cases, were never preserved). Instead, the radio sound scholar is largely compelled to rely on secondhand textual descriptions of voices instead of hearing those voices firsthand. There are some exceptions of course; we can hear and see Elvira Ríos, for example, and as a result we can appreciate the androgynous qualities of her voice. However, when *Antena* editors complained about men singing "women's songs" in 1932; when De Paoli excoriated the radioteatro for its shrill, nerve-wracking, and hysterical vocalizations; and when the *Manual de radiodifusión* issued a prohibition on "effeminate distortions" on the airwaves, we can only speculate as to what those vocalizations sounded like and how often they were heard on Argentine airwaves.

Despite these limitations, this material nevertheless allows us to bring a sonic dimension to Garber's ideas about transvestism and category crisis, and it invites us to think more substantively about the complicated relationships among voice, body, and gender and the conceptions of vocal heteronormativity, especially as it relates to radio speech. There seems little question that radio's emergence, in intersection with other challenges to existing social hierarchies afoot at the time, combined to produce the kind of "category crisis" in which one might expect the transvestite to make his/her appearance. A medium of massification and democratization of culture, but also of contagion and transgression, radio was an ideal vessel for the cultivation of anxieties about transvestism and gender ambiguity. Fears that radio might surreptitiously introduce homoerotic desire or normalize transgendered performances or identity were not merely about gender and sexuality; they were the focal point for diffuse concerns that the historical moment was shaking loose old social structures and cultural boundaries. For some, the radio transvestite was a convenient caricature, embodying all the forces that seemed to be turning previously solid ground into shifting sands.

The Media of Politics

3

HOW TO DO THINGS WITH WAVES

United States Radio and Latin America in
the Times of the Good Neighbor

Gisela Cramer

*"When a million or more people hear the same subject matter, the same
arguments and appeals, the same music and humor, when their attention
is held in the same way and at the same time to the same stimuli, it is
psychologically inevitable that they should acquire in some degree common
interests, common tastes, and common attitudes. In short, it seems to be the
nature of radio to encourage people to think and feel alike."*

Gordon W. Allport and Hadley Cantril, *The Psychology of Radio*

IN THEIR PIONEERING study *The Psychology of Radio*, Gordon W. Allport and
Hadley Cantril venture that radio had profound effects on audiences: radio
encouraged people to "think and feel alike." "More than any other medium
of communication," they suggest, radio "is capable of forming a crowd
mind among individuals who are physically separated from one another."[1]
Few historians and media analysts today would follow the stimulus-
response model that informed the research approach of the two psychologists, nor would they subscribe to the conceptualizations employed,
but what has continued to be of central interest to communications scholars and historians alike is the capacity of radio and other mass media to
generate what Benedict Anderson calls "imagined communities."[2] Paddy

Scannell coined an analogous term—"we-ness"—and refers to the capacity of the mass media to create a "public, shared and sociable world-in-common."[3] The precise mechanisms at work remain far from clear, but it seems that this capacity relies, to some extent, on the fact that modern broadcasting technologies mimic a host of social institutions that structure human interaction and provide a sense of belonging. In a 1936 broadcast, the United States Federal Communications Commissioner Anning S. Prall hailed radio "as a combination of the schoolhouse, the church, the public rostrum, the newspaper, the theater, the concert hall."[4] Social historians would add the sport stadium, the pub, the kitchen, and other spaces of everyday encounters to this list.

Whereas this "world-in-common," particularly as mediated by radio, may have an intensely local flavor, the modern mass media are usually credited for their capacity to generate imagined communities on a larger scale. David Morley and Kevin Robins explain: "The 'magic carpet' of broadcasting technologies has played a fundamental role in promoting national unity at a symbolic level, linking individuals and their families to the centres of national life, offering the audience an image of itself and of the nation as a knowable community, a wider, public world beyond the routines of a narrow existence."[5] In a similar vein, Jesus Martín-Barbero credits modern broadcasting technologies in Latin America with the achievement of transmuting "the political idea of the nation into lived experience, into sentiment and into the quotidian."[6] Earlier on, and in analyzing more tangible conditions for the emergence of nationalities, sociologist Karl Deutsch proposed that the "range and effectiveness" of internal communications was an important factor in differentiating one country from another.[7]

As Benedict Anderson observes for the print media during earlier stages of nation building,[8] radio's role in this process was not necessarily an intentional or premeditated one. In the United States, profit expectations were driving networks to expand their reach into every corner of the nation's vast territory, thereby increasingly addressing audiences on a national scale. Still, the daily experience of hearing seemingly innocuous phrases such as "This program is coming to you over a coast-to-coast network," Allport and Cantril suggest, "inevitably increases our sense of membership in the national family."[9] Commercial interests led U.S. broadcasters to increasingly dedicate space to popular sport events and other mass attractions, but, as Susan Douglas has argued more recently, by doing so, they engaged millions in cognitive and emotional activities that shaped "a sense of national culture."[10]

Radio's modes to evoke "we-ness," in order to be successful, had to respond to intersubjective expectations and thus went well beyond the simple stimulus-response model suggested by early communication scholars. Capturing audiences required broadcasters to literally listen to their listeners. Indeed, even when broadcasting systems followed state imperatives and rather self-consciously took on the role of instilling a sense of national identity, as did the British Empire Service among (white) compatriots throughout far-flung colonies, their aural representations of home and nation were not necessarily the product of top-down decision-making processes. As Emma Robertson suggests, the success of the Empire Service rested not least on its ability to tap into listeners' desires and their notions of what "home" and "nation" were all about.[11]

Nonetheless, during the 1930s and early 1940s, radio's role in the construction of imagined communities became an increasingly deliberate and top-down affair, even when broadcasting remained in private hands and pursued largely commercial interests, as was the case in the United States. "Radio was seized upon by national governments . . . as a primary nation-building tool," Michele Hilmes concludes. "It became the chosen medium of national identity formation in a troubled time, as the reconstruction of the 1920s gave way to political unrest and depression economics, and then again to wartime mobilization. Thus the construction of radio as a medium remains almost synonymous with the construction of twentieth-century national identities, not only in the U.S. and Western Europe but across the globe."[12] As such, radio became an important part of (what Orvar Lofgren called) the "micro-physics of learning to belong to the nation-as-home" and thus contributed to a "cultural thickening" of the nation state.[13]

This invitation of "learning to belong," however, is not directed at all listeners in the same way. More so, the "we-ness" constructed by the media, as the critics of Paddy Scannell point out, is not an imagined community open to all.[14] If radio in the United States helped to assimilate a plethora of immigrant communities, it did so "under the cultural sign and sound of whiteness."[15] Radio may be a "blind" medium, but it was not "colorblind," and racialized stereotypes of the *other* served to sharply delimit the boundaries of "we-ness." Rather than conceptualizing the community-creating capacities of the media along a simple binary in/out divide, however, it is probably more accurate to think in terms of a less rigid model.

Intent on capturing mass audiences, broadcasts tended to follow the main-stream. As such, they reflected a socially and ethnically stratified, as well as deeply gendered, society, thereby reproducing restrictive notions of citizenship that did not confer equal standing for all. Embedded in deeply ingrained structures of inequality, such restrictive notions of citizenship tend to be "sticky." Yet for one reason or another, they may change or oscillate over time.

Thus, as many scholars have observed, toward the late 1930s and amid increasing anxieties about national cohesiveness and the coming of war, radio in the United States came to be used as a medium to communicate broader and more inclusive representations of nationhood. Cued by government agencies and civic organizations, the networks incorporated programs that were meant to embrace and instill respect for ethnic and religious minorities.[16] Programs such as *Americans All — Immigrants All*, sponsored by the Office of Education, celebrated the contributions of African Americans, Jews, and other minorities to the progress and well-being of the nation.[17] During the war years, this zest for inclusiveness intensified, at least in its breadth. "It is fair to say," two media analysts concluded in 1946, "that there remains no minority group that has not been represented, directly or indirectly, on the radio."[18] Although stereotyping comments or jokes at the expense of minorities by no means disappeared from the airwaves, wartime radio paid homage to a more inclusive and broader conception of citizenship.[19]

What is less known is that this quest for unity was not limited to the national arena. Toward the late 1930s and, particularly, during the war years, radio output in the United States changed markedly with respect to Latin America. Broadcasters, both large and small, engaged in a variety of strategies that invited U.S. audiences not just to acquaint themselves with the good neighbors to the south but also to imagine themselves as part of a wider, Pan-American world and community of nations. This is the theme to be explored in this chapter.

Imagined Communities and Pan-American Imaginings: Educational, News, and Commentary Programs

Such efforts to use radio as a means to further Pan-Americanism were not altogether new. The Pan-American Union, for example, had long sought to use radio as a unifying force by acquainting North and South

Americans with one another's cultural accomplishments. Apart from occasional broadcasts of concerts or lectures, however, little had come of these initiatives.[20] The broadcasting industry had shown little interest in inter-American affairs, even as renderings of Latin American popular music came to be highly appreciated among mass audiences. Several famous radio orchestras of the era did incorporate tangos or rumbas into their repertoires, but such appropriations of Latin America's popular culture in itself had done little to promote an interest in the region. In terms of news coverage, for example, Latin America had remained rather marginal on the U.S. airwaves.[21]

Toward the end of the 1930s, however, and under subtle pressure by the government,[22] the broadcasting industry started to produce Pan-American imaginings with a clear mission and increasing zeal. The genre that most clearly reflected the good-neighborly zeitgeist of the 1930s was the educational program. The first major production was *Brave New World* (1937–1938), a program that playfully appropriated the title of Aldous Huxley's famous novel. It aimed to acquaint audiences in the United States with "the story of Latin America. . . . Twenty nations with a history and culture to be admired and a democratic ideal we share." Produced by Columbia Broadcasting Systems (CBS) in cooperation with the Office of Education, the State Department, and a staff of experts directed by Samuel Guy Inman, the series consisted of twenty-six programs built around lively portraits. It avoided stuffy facts and dreary figures and started out with a "blood and thunder" script on the adventures of conquistadors Pizarro, Cortés, and Balboa. Education commissioner John W. Studebaker proclaimed, "This will probably be the first time in history that one government has spent time and money on a sustained effort to help its own citizens appreciate the ideals of people across the border."[23] Broadcast over a nationwide network of more than one hundred stations, *Brave New World* made a considerable splash. At universities, schools, and educational forums, listening groups discussed the series, and many schools requested scripts for the drama to be reenacted by pupils. More than 70,000 listeners wrote to the Office of Education and requested informational leaflets and bibliographies for the series.[24]

With the coming of war, Latin American contents increased markedly, not only in the educational genre. This was partly the doing of the government and, more particularly, of Nelson A. Rockefeller's Office of Inter-American Affairs (OIAA),[25] which pressured both the large networks and the plethora of smaller independent stations into broadcasting contents with a Pan-American spin. No less important, broadcasters also responded to a growing interest in inter-American affairs among wider audiences.

Events in Europe had shocked U.S. citizens into a state of alert. By 1940, as ever larger territories were falling into the orbit of the Nazi empire and clouds of war and aggression were thickening in the Pacific, the world seemed to be closing in on the United States. For sure, the public was deeply divided on the question of whether their country should enter the war. But many on both sides of the divide had become convinced that the situation required embracing their good neighbors to the south into a firm alliance of New World nations and that failure to do so would jeopardize national security.[26] "Affection for Latin Americans has broken out like a speckled rash on the skin of the North American body politic," quipped historian Hubert Herring in 1941, and "club-women read papers on the Humboldt Current, dress up as Aymarás, listen to guitarists strum tunes reputed to come from the Amazon. College presidents substitute courses on the Incas for those on the age of Pericles. Chambers of Commerce give dinners to visiting Argentine bankers, and keep up a set of twenty-one American flags among their props. Schoolgirls cut paper dolls which represent the dwellers by Atitlán."[27]

Radio responded but also contributed to the "rash." Latin American affairs became an important item in leading news and commentary programs,[28] and larger networks sent correspondents to report from the spot.[29] Smaller stations used a conveniently prepared news roundup delivered by the press agencies, *News of the Other Americas*.[30] This was not just about news and information, as the programs prepared by Edward Tomlinson, the leading commentator on Latin American affairs with the National Broadcasting Corporation (NBC), suggest. Tomlinson sought not only to inform but also to educate his fellow citizens. A tireless advocate of Latin America's importance for national security, Tomlinson sought to persuade his listeners that the time had come to scrap their "superiority complex" and learn more about their neighbors to the south.[31]

Spanish language programs, previously found on the schedules of regional or educational stations, now entered the larger commercial circuits. The most noticeable production was *Down Mexico Way*, a weekly program that combined Spanish lessons with the objective of acquainting listeners with Mexico's diverse musical and cultural heritage. Built around the adventures of a young student traveling south of the border, the program was produced by NBC at the instigation of Vice President Henry A. Wallace. One of the most fervent advocates of the Good Neighbor policy, Wallace himself had started to learn Spanish and, as *Time* had it, "Like many a language student before him, he discovered that songs improve the ear, enlarge the vocabulary and warm the heart."[32] The OIAA's analysts took a rather dim view of the show, rating it as "very, very poor" and "patronizing."[33] Nevertheless, *Down Mexico Way*, launched in February 1942 with a considerable publicity campaign and accompanied by free booklets, turned out to be rather successful. In response to popular demand for an extension of the show, NBC produced a follow-up, and by June 1942 its cast was now heard exploring other countries of the region for *Pan American Holiday*.[34]

During the war, however, many educational programs attempted more than to "warm the heart." They insisted on projecting an "epic of a greater America," to borrow a Boltonian term,[35] a master narrative that dwelled on a shared heritage, on common struggles and interests. Such were the themes that surfaced in the productions of the *American School of the Air,* the flagship of educational broadcasting maintained by CBS. By 1940, the "world's largest classroom" had metamorphosed into the *American School of the Air.* Taken with its new mission to advance hemisphere unity, and with support from Rockefeller's OIAA, it set out with five weekly programs built around the history, geography, literature, and music, as well as social, political, and economic problems of South, Central, and North America. Lectures were accompanied by dramatizations such as *This Living World,* which helped students process the content, and teachers were supplied with free manuals. According to contemporary estimates, some eight million school children heard these programs with some regularity.[36] CBS, moreover, made strenuous efforts to build a Pan-American network of learning. In 1941, the *American School of the Air* organized two Pan-American conferences in—Atlantic City and Mexico City—which brought together government officials, broadcasters, and centers of learning.[37] It had programs and teaching materials translated into Spanish and Portuguese and was made available to CBS affiliates throughout the Americas.[38]

Not to be left behind, in April 1942, NBC announced a far-reaching project that invited broadcasters and institutions of higher learning throughout the hemisphere to participate in the programming of its new *Inter-American University of the Air.* This broadly conceived project drew on the expertise of well-known musicologists, historians, and writers from the United States and resulted in a number of outstanding series.

Music of the New World, for example, presented thirty-six half-hour broadcasts that traced chronologically the development of music in the Western Hemisphere from pre-Columbian times to the present. Although insisting that the aim was not to suggest "hemispheric isolationism," the producers did express "the belief that the development of music in this hemisphere can only be appreciated in its true significance when it is related to the background of life and history in the Americas."[39] *American Story,* a cycle conceived by Archibald MacLeish, Librarian of Congress and Pulitzer Prize–winning poet, spun a greater American saga from the times of conquest to the present where, in the words of MacLeish, "from Alaska to the tip of South America, every stage of life was the same."[40] Thus, while exploring the conquest of the Americas, the series highlighted the experience of European settlers and their struggle to survive in the vastness and hostile environment of an unknown continent, an experience that would set their civilization apart from the Old World and that would ultimately and inevitably lead to the wars of independence. Another cycle, *Lands of the Free,* equally celebrated the shared heritage of the Americas. It dwelled on the experience of colonialism and the struggles for independence and on other topics that, conveniently framed, could serve as a historical analogy for the current need for a Pan-American front against dangers emanating from overseas.[41]

Rebranding the Latins—Propaganda and Realpolitik

Such major educational ventures, as undertaken by CBS or NBC, involved production costs that smaller, independent stations were unable to shell out. The latter, however, could resort to materials that were supplied to them free of charge by Rockefeller's OIAA. Among the more notable of such endeavors was the weekly *Salute* series, which the OIAA supplied to some 850 local stations throughout the nation since the middle of 1941.[42] The *Salute* series featured individual Latin American countries and was broadcast on national holidays, the birthdays of past and present statesmen, during important state visits, or on any other occasion that allowed for a subject treatment with a Pan-American spin. The fifteen-minute programs consisted of ready-made scripts and included recommendations for the music to be used as well as phonetic transcriptions for the correct pronunciation of Spanish, Portuguese, or French names and terms. Typically, they contained information on the geographical location, size, and topography of the countries in question and dwelled heavily on their importance for the U.S. war economy and national security. Without the assistance of the good neighbors to the south, these programs insinuated, the United States was not going to win the war. More than friendly allies, these good neighbors were featured as sister republics—belonging to a family of nations and therefore worthy of respect and special consideration. As such, *Salute* emphasized similarities rather than differences, closeness rather than distance. In order to make Latin America intelligible to domestic audiences, the programs referred to subject matters that could be framed in terms that were both familiar and comforting to listeners.

Thus, *Salute* portrayed Latin America's heroes of independence, a heavily worked theme, as standing shoulder to shoulder with George Washington and other familiar figures—a Pan-American pantheon of heroes who fought for the same ideals and shared the same qualities.[43] If the grand narrative of U.S. history gave a special place to those forefathers who, like Abraham Lincoln, had risen from a humble background to reach the pinnacle of power by virtue of their intelligence, hard work, and civic spirit, these programs portrayed Latin American statesmen, past and present, in similar terms, whenever possible. These personal portraits avoided discussing race or using racializing attributes and thereby implicitly "whitened" their subjects. Not surprisingly, perhaps, some of the contemporary heads of state from the sister republics came to be introduced as southern counterparts to Franklin D. Roosevelt.[44]

If, in earlier days, the North American gaze had exposed a marked interest in South America's political institutions as a benchmark for civilization and progress and, more often than not, had found them wanting,[45] the *Salute* programs sought to diminish the perception of a civilizatory gap between the north and south. They highlighted similarities in constitutions and legal systems; they dwelled on the great strides made in primary education or public housing; they marveled about splendid highways and modern architecture; and they insinuated that in more than one respect Latin America's institutional progress had actually predated developments in North America.[46] "The Cubans are progressive in every way"[47]—such or similar phrases are to be found in just about every *Salute* program produced by the OIAA.[48] Even seemingly innocuous statements about the climate, for example, were clearly destined to destabilize common preconceptions that stood in the way of sympathetic understanding. Thus, against commonly held notions of the tropics as a breeding ground for disease, poverty,

and lethargy, the *Salute to Cuba* found the island to have a "delightful climate the year 'round" and indeed rather superior to the United States since
"there is never the enervating humidity to be found during the summer
months in some of our North American cities."[49]

If the *Salute* programs followed the same overarching objectives as
the educational broadcasts previously discussed, they set about their task
in an unabashedly propagandistic fashion. Schooled in the ways of advertisement, the *Salute* scriptwriters in the employ of the Rockefeller office
followed strategies not unlike today's national rebranding campaigns. As
such, their country profiles simply omitted any information at odds with
their objective. Deeply embedded in the exigencies of realpolitik, moreover, they did not shy away from concocting glossy portrayals of petty dic-
tators and strongmen who, though falling short of Franklin D. Roosevelt's
Four Freedoms, were found to be highly cooperative with regard to the war
effort. Thus, more than one program hailed Fulgencio Batista not just as a
valuable ally but also as an admirable statesman. His life story was found to
"read like a story of Horatio Alger." Born into a humble family, Batista rose
by his own merits, "not unlike our own Abraham Lincoln," and he thus
demonstrated "the unlimited opportunities that exist for all men who live
in a free country, where ability, initiative and ambition receive their just
rewards." Government policies under Batista were presented as resem-
bling the New Deal—Cuban style. Perhaps needless to say, no mention
was made on the peculiar way that FOOL-HÉN-SEE-O BAH-TÉES-TA
had gained his power.[50]

Of course, not all the series produced on behalf of the OIAA took on
such a stark flavor. "We, men and women of the Americas, came together
out of a common heritage, a tradition planted a hundred years deep. We
were born out of Revolution, all twenty-one of us," explained Orson
Welles in *Hello Americans* (CBS 1942–1943). "It's the sameness I'm talking
about, sameness in spite of difference. Different sounds to the words, but
the same idea. Different colors, but the same spirit. Different churches, but
the same faith." Before this could sound too portentous, he added, "Different liquor, but the same hangover."[51] Welles had just returned from Rio de
Janeiro where he had been engaged in a film project that had failed to come
to fruition. He had insisted on placing dark-skinned Brazilians from the
favelas at the center of his film, a proposition that antagonized not just his
employers at RKO but also Brazilian censorship officials who wished to see
their country portrayed in a rather different manner. No such difficulties

arose with the OIAA. "Nelson Rockefeller," reported *Time*, "trusts Welles so completely that he does not even go over the South American scripts."[52] *Hello Americans* started out with a feature on Brazilian music, costarring the wildly popular Carmen Miranda, before branching out into a variety of topics related to Latin America and inter-American affairs. "Welles took seriously his responsibilities as a roving ambassador for Pan-Americanism, a role in perfect accord with his personal sympathies and his left-leaning politics," film historian Robert Stam observes.[53] Stam and others rightfully stress Welles's sensibilities to class and racial issues—sensibilities that gave his approach to hemisphere unity a distinct and somewhat subversive flavor. Nevertheless, even the Welles brand of Pan-Americanism did not wholly escape wartime realpolitik from creeping in. This is visible not least in the radio programs on Brazil. As part of the OIAA's policy to honor South American heads of state, Welles took an active part in introducing President Getúlio Vargas and his *Estado Novo* in very favorable terms to mass audiences in the United States. In this role, he orchestrated a musical extravaganza, interwoven with congratulatory speeches, to celebrate Vargas's birthday in April 1942. Originating from the famous Urca Casino in Rio de Janeiro, the show was broadcast by local stations in Brazil and transmitted to coast-to-coast audiences in the United States. Few foreign statesmen had been feasted in this manner. Not surprisingly, Vargas and his Ministry for Propaganda were delighted.[54]

Entertainment

If the gospel of Pan-Americanism is most easily observable in education and related genres, wartime entertainment shows also contributed their share. This was partly due to the fact that the government, in order to reach larger audiences, did not shy away from sponsoring entertainment. The most enduring of such shows was *Adventures of the Sea Hound,* a dramatic serial for children produced on behalf of the OIAA. Broadcast fives times a week over the Blue Network from 1942 to 1945, it featured Captain Silver and his sidekick Jerry hunting Nazi spies throughout the hemisphere.[55] Adult listeners would learn about Latin America's history, geography, natural resources, and importance for the U.S. war economy in *Ripley's Believe It or Not.* One of the most successful shows in the quiz genre, *Ripley's* continued to specialize, as it had done in the 1930s, in the unusual and bizarre. During the war and under contract with the

OIAA, however, it now addressed topics that would further hemisphere unity.[56]

Such outright government sponsorship, however, was the exception. More common was the insertion of government-produced materials with a Pan-American spin into established shows under commercial sponsorship. Rockefeller's OIAA released thousands of such items, and cooperation with networks and advertisement agencies was rather fluid.[57] Some of the OIAA's leading officers had occupied important positions in the radio and advertisement industry before the war. This organizational interface greatly facilitated interaction with the private sector.[58] Thus, Dupont's *Cavalcade of America,* a rather successful dramatic anthology that employed some of the most promising young playwrights of the era and featured top stars from Broadway and Hollywood, branched out to include Pan-American content material, prepared by none other than Orson Welles.[59] The Coca-Cola company agreed to include salutes to the good-neighbor presidents in a prime-time program featuring light classical music, orchestral versions of popular songs, and Broadway tunes. *André Kostelanetz Presents* henceforth presented, on a bimonthly schedule, the favorite song of a Latin American president, starting with Mexico's Ávila Camacho and "Incertidumbre." The following salutes included "The Lovely Girls of Bahia" (for Getúlio Vargas) and "Siboney" (for Fulgencio Batista).[60]

The quantity of such program insertions increased markedly on certain days of the year, particularly around Pan American Day (April 14). In 1942, for instance, the OIAA was reported to have been successful in introducing material on the subject of Pan-Americanism into a wide variety of shows on and around April 14, including commentary programs, variety and human interests programs, and comedy and quiz shows.[61] At least in 1942, it seems, U.S. audiences could hardly escape Pan American Day.

Pressured by the government and responding to audience interests, moreover, the networks produced a variety of sustaining programs entirely devoted to Pan-American themes. These usually provided music and light entertainment, and they often included informational material and short dramatizations. CBS led the way with *Calling Pan America* (1941–1942). It connected with a different capital city every week, featuring outstanding local artists but also brief addresses by government officials.[62] Not to be outdone, NBC came up with *Good Neighbors* (1941), a dramatized human interest program that dealt with both historical and present themes and was usually built around a particular country.[63] It was written by Wyllis Cooper, a veteran radio dramaturge who had previously produced and directed *Lights Out*, "the most goose-fleshing chiller-dillers in air history."[64] Intent on producing cutting-edge entertainment, NBC also "threw in Dr. Frank Black and his sixty-piece orchestra, a troop of some twenty actors and the gilt-edged intonings of Announcer Milton Cross."[65] CBS, meanwhile, had revamped its standing orchestra under conductor Alfredo Antonini as the Pan American Orchestra. The latter cooperated with a range of outstanding musicians and singers from Latin America, including Mexican tenors Nestor Mesta Chaires and Juan Arvizu, Argentine composer and arranger Terig Tucci, or Puerto Rican vocalist Elsa Miranda. Alfredo Antonini and his Pan American Orchestra provided the core for *Viva America,* a program that survived into the early postwar years.[66] These and other shows, including *Hemisphere Review,*[67] *Saludos Amigos* (NBC), *Romance of Latin America* (CBS),[68] *Brazilian Parade,* and *The Americas Speak* (Mutual Broadcasting System—MBS), gave Latin American artists and music a presence never enjoyed before on U.S. airwaves.[69]

What did such shows convey? The available evidence is less than satisfactory, but the remaining fragments suggest that many of them addressed Good Neighbor themes rather explicitly and that their choice of content was meant not only to entertain but also to instill sympathy with and respect for Latin America. They therefore stressed the nationality of the artists involved and referred to their country of origin in congratulatory terms.[70] The networks, moreover, were keen on portraying Latin American talents not only in the crowd-pleasing slots but also in those reserved for more sophisticated or serious artistic expressions. Incidentally, the artists thus honored did not necessarily appreciate their being introduced to U.S. audiences on the Good Neighbor ticket. "In Europe," composer Heitor Villa-Lobos once complained, "I am known as Villa-Lobos. In the United States I am only a Brazilian—applauded because of the Good Neighbor policy."[71] Still, as Antonio Pedro Tota observes, wartime radio gave a "touch of refinement to the image of Brazil."[72] Indeed, this "touch of refinement" was not restricted to Brazil.

At the same time, however, the broadcasting industry's approach to Pan-American entertainment also drew on deeply ingrained mechanisms of othering. To quote from a sequence closing one of the many *Adventures of the Sea Hound:* "Once again, Captain Silver has broken up a Nazi ring. Once again, he is responsible for ridding Latin America of the Nazi menace and helping to unite all of the Americas in the gigantic task of defeating the Axis."[73] Once again, we may add, the Latin characters in the plot were depicted as sympathetic yet hapless victims who needed to be rescued by a manly hero from the north. Elsewhere—and not surprisingly, given the long-standing tradition of depicting inter-American relations in gendered terms—stereotypes of the sensual Latin female broke through and visions of hemisphere unity could easily take an erotic turn. "You are a dream man, Rudy," flirted Brazilian singer Carmen Miranda with entertainer Rudy Vallee over the ether. "Would you like to make love with me?" Rudy did not dare, of course, but instead evaded by referring to the big Good Neighbor picture: "Our two countries could have better relations after our marriage."[74] Such scenes were not limited to artists representing popular genres. In analyzing programs featuring Brazilian soprano Elsie Houston, for example, Tota finds her to be represented as the "more erudite" version of "the same sensuality."[75]

If wartime radio sought to present Latin America and its citizens as part of a family of nations that deserved special consideration and respect, it also exposed content material that depicted the *other* Americans in rather different terms than the national "we." Although, as we have seen earlier, some broadcasting genres dwelled heavily on a discourse of sameness, visions of difference did creep in, particularly in the entertainment genre.[76] The imagined community U.S. audiences were invited to picture themselves as being part of, after all, was a stratified one that gave differential standing to its constitutive parts. Such visions of a stratified Pan-American community translated hegemonic pretensions into a popular language to be disseminated by the mass media.

Flying to Rio (and Elsewhere)

"We may go where we wish when we wish—all we have to do is to say so," the BBC's Donald McWhinnie once remarked when referring to the peculiar ability of the "blind" medium to take its listeners on imaginary journeys to different places, near and far, without much ado.[77] If Edward R. Murrow's famous live broadcasts led mass audiences into the horrors of the London Blitz and other theaters of war, many a trip undertaken by wartime radio in the United States was actually going off into a different direction, that is, down Mexico way and farther south.[78]

Orson Welles's lively portraits of the Caribbean in *Hello Americans* thus took listeners "hopping around the islands between the American continents, offering a kind of sound-illustrated lecture on history, geography, economics, politics and mere human interest."[79] *Adventures of the Sea Hound* enacted a visit to a different country every show. In order to help its young listeners visualize the hemisphere and grasp the strategic importance of the sister republics, NBC encouraged listeners to request complementary materials such as the *Captain Silver's Sea Chart*—a colorful map of the Americas that identified the most important products and carried pictures of outstanding heroes and flags of all the Latin American republics.[80]

"Good evening, good evening, good neighbors. . . . Now we will fly to Rio de Janeiro," exclaimed entertainer Rudy Vallee as he invited his listeners on a "good will tour to Brazil."[81] Such invitations, of course, were fictional since listeners did not leave their homes. Indeed, Vallee himself did not have to leave his studio in order to flirt with Carmen Miranda. Quite a few of the programs with a Pan-American spin, however, did originate from south of the border or incorporate retransmissions from broadcasting stations in Latin America. "This is Orson Welles, speaking from South America, from Rio de Janeiro, in the United States of Brazil"—a voice over the ether opened the aural doors to the Urca Casino, where listeners would attend Getúlio Vargas's birthday party. "This show is for all his friends. From Maine to Manaus, from São Paulo to Chicago, from São Salvador to San Francisco. This is being transmitted over most stations of Brazil and over a hundred stations in America."[82]

On a range of special occasions, the large networks retransmitted specially arranged programs. Pan American Day is a case in point. For instance, in 1942, CBS arranged a special Pan American Day program in cooperation with the OIAA, featuring Brazilian soprano Olga Coelho and other outstanding artists, as well as salutes from government officials transmitted simultaneously from Rio de Janeiro and Washington.[83] Shared religious holidays provided another occasion for such specially arranged programs. Thus, in 1943, CBS produced an Easter Sunday special that had Andre Kostelanetz conducting the ninety-piece Mexican symphonic orchestra. Produced with the support of the OIAA, it also featured two distinguished Mexican opera singers, contralto Toña La Negra and tenor Nestor Mesta Chaires. In order to increase the authenticity of the listening experience, program arrangements added additional elements to the particular sound-scape. In this case, listeners would hear the ringing of the bells from the shrine of the Virgen de Guadalupe.[84]

Other programs incorporated retransmissions on a regular basis. *Calling Pan America*, for instance, connected to a different Latin American capital every week by hooking up with a local station of the CBS inter-American network *La Cadena de las Américas*. NBC had similar arrangements with stations affiliated to its *Cadena Panamericana*, as did MBS for programs such as *The Americas Speak* or *Brazilian Parade*.[85]

A rather peculiar case of Pan-American wanderings was *Vox pop*. One of the most long-standing quiz shows on the air, it specialized in im-promptu interviews and mildly provoking questions (e.g., "How many feathers has a hen?"). In previous years, *Vox pop*'s presenters had criss-crossed the national territory, making it one of the most peripatetic shows on the air. In 1941, it became the first commercial quiz show in the United States to originate from south of the Rio Grande, as the presenters took their microphones to Mexico, Cuba, and Puerto Rico. In this case, however, interaction with Latin American citizens was avoided, no doubt for fears that the kind of humor exposed by Parks Johnson and Wally Butterworth might provoke adverse reactions among the uninitiated. "*Vox pop* is tak-ing no chances with the Good Neighbor Policy" reported the *New York Times*. Interviews were restricted to members of the American colony and selected officials.[86]

As communications researchers and media historians have suggested, radio—despite its "blindness"—can create or deepen a sense of territorial space. In many countries, particularly during the 1930s and 1940s, and in a more or less deliberate way, this capacity was harnessed to create a sense of belonging to a clearly demarcated territory: the nation-as-home.[87] War-time radio in the United States embarked on voyages that were mapping out the hemisphere as a habitat for a different kind of imagined community on a Pan-American scale.

Looking back

"This is a South American year," *Washington Post* journalist Katherine Graham announced in March 1941, as the Pan American Union, supported by the government and by hundreds of civic organizations throughout the United States, was gearing up for Pan American Day celebrations. "You are learning Spanish if you don't know it already. You talk with familiarity of Caracas and Santiago. You are up to date or should be—on problems of trade and diplomacy between the continents. And if you can sing, it's Carmen Miranda's 'South American Way.'"[88] This popular tune, of course, had little to do with Latin America,[89] but what mattered—and this was the gist of Graham's article—was something else: the imagination.

Indeed, Latin America had captured the popular imagination, and this upsurge of interest showed some very visible and even quantifiable effects. During the war, requests for informational materials prepared by the Pan American Union and other agencies increased markedly, as hundreds of civic organizations, including women's clubs, chapters of the YMCA, Rotary, and the American Legion, set out to organize lectures, exhibitions, and other events. Towns and cities engaged in organizing fiestas around Latin American themes,[90] and schools and universities throughout the nation reported a growing demand for Spanish and, to a lesser extent, Portuguese language courses. Whereas Spanish authors such as Cervantes had reigned supreme on the syllabi of the Spanish literature curriculum, Latin American authors were now read with awe.[91] Such examples abound.

By and large, however, this was a mood that was not destined to last. Born as it was out of national anxieties produced by economic depression and the coming of war, it was not to withstand the tides of time, though it did hold on a little longer than conditions in the real world might have suggested. Indeed, the idea that the future and greatness of the United States was inextricably bound to the fate of the "other" Americas was most forcefully promoted at a time when U.S. policy makers were turning their attentions elsewhere. "With the involvement of the United States in World War II," historian Donald M. Dozer observes, "the primacy of Latin America in the policy and planning of the Roosevelt administration was abandoned."[92] As the United States started to face the challenges of the postwar world, Latin America shrank to a rather marginal dot on the new landscape of national anxieties and concerns.

As the war was drawing to a close, radio's quest for inclusiveness withered away, and it wasn't limited to the inter-American front. "Never before in the history of network broadcasting had racial issues been probed so openly," concludes William Barlow, "but even as global victory was at hand, the discussion of race relations and the emphasis on black programming was disappearing from the American airwaves."[93] Reviewing postwar programming on both radio and television, Michele Hilmes observes that "little of the wartime renegotiation of black representation can be perceived."[94]

There are good reasons to assume that radio and the mass media in general contributed significantly to the way Latin America was perceived by the public at large and, more specifically, by those who had little knowledge of, or experience with, the region and its inhabitants.[95] More to the point, empirical research undertaken on behalf of the OIAA suggested that radio could be harnessed to bring about a more positive disposition toward Latin America. A regional radio project undertaken by the University of Texas in the summer of 1941 (*Know Your Neighbor*), that combined informational and entertainment programs about past and present Mexico, with surveys on the attitudes of listeners toward Mexico, gave rise to cautious optimism.[96] Public opinion polls conducted during the war did indeed suggest that the attitudes of U.S. citizens toward the good neighbors to the south were brightening up somewhat.[97] However, there is no way of gauging the net effect of U.S. radio's newfound, if short-lived, infatuation with Latin America.

U.S. radio during the times of the Good Neighbor invited U.S. audiences to imagine themselves as part of a wider, Pan-American world and community of nations. Such broadcasts with a Pan-American spin increased markedly with the coming of war and were intent on instilling sympathy with, and respect for, Latin America. Much of the more consciously arranged programming dwelled heavily on a discourse of sameness, but—as is more easily observable in the various entertainment genres discussed here—notions of difference nevertheless crept in. Ultimately, this imagined community on a Pan-American scale was a stratified one in which leadership fell to U.S. citizens or, more precisely, men.

4

WEAPONS OF THE GEEK

Romantic Narratives, Sonic Technologies,
and Tinkerers in 1930s Santiago, Cuba

Alejandra Bronfman

IN 1923, A columnist in Santiago de Cuba's *La Independencia* applauded the achievements of a sound medium, the telegraph, noting that "with its magic touch it has eliminated the isolation and loneliness in the middle of the sea and in deserted places." With emphasis on the isolation felt in a small city, especially in an island nation, the author relished the ways an array of sonic technologies created new roles and capacities for sound. The column also noted the progression from telegraph to telephone, culminating with the latest invention, radiotelephony, which broadcast radio programs through telephone wires. This, the author proposed, offered not just the wonder of "Hertzian waves that are the invisible messengers of human thought," but more practically, "the solution for education within nations."[1] Santiago's connections to the media that delivered sound would be transformative, he predicted, in many spheres of daily life. Sound would propagate education and cultural understanding, assuage class differences as both the wealthy and the not so wealthy enjoyed broadcasts of music or sports in the comfort of their homes, and prevent accidents or provide aid during natural disasters.[2]

The writer was silent, however, about the role of sonic technologies in political struggles. Yet, as Friedrich Kittler points out, telegraph and wireless radio emerged as part of military endeavors to improve communications in wartime.[3] Admittedly, this was a less bucolic use of mediated sound that lent itself more to the vocabularies of conflict and repression than of harmony and wonder. The information conveyed through wires or over airwaves, after all, might divide and threaten as easily as it might unify and uplift. One of the episodes I will take up in this chapter involves a youth who was arrested because he "had knowledge of telegraphy."[4] As such, it speaks to an alternative, equally powerful understanding of technology. If some residents of Santiago seemed enthralled with the possibilities offered by new media, others were attendant to the possibilities for sabotage and subversion, especially in the hands of those with some knowledge of how these new devices operated.

Both the optimistic and the suspicious views are rooted in a shared romance of technology and modernity. In *Technoromanticism: Digital Narrative, Holism, and the Romance of the Real,* Richard Coyne argues that communications technologies are often the subject of romantic, teleological narratives of progress, which produce "a surplus of expectation." These narratives grant extensive powers to sound, making it not just an actor in a variety of scenarios but a heroic one, working to soothe, instruct, deliver vital information, or save lives. They also involve a "quest for unity," imagining for media the power to create and transform communities.[5] In many cases, narratives about communications technologies imagine that they deliver liberation in some form, be it from isolation, or parochialism, or sheer loneliness. By the same token, one community's salvation could be another's downfall. Even so, a narrative presuming the power of technology remains.

Historians of the Caribbean have become attuned to romantic narratives in part due to David Scott's evaluations of their implications.[6] Romantic accounts of revolution, such as those found in C. L. R. James's early edition of *Black Jacobins,* may have served to rouse nations on the brink of decolonization, inspiring the nationalist impetus as well as the makers of memory in subsequent generations.[7] Yet, argues Scott, the postcolonial present is not particularly well served by romantic narratives that clearly distinguish good from bad, darkness from light, and control from revolt.

The promises they made have gone largely unfulfilled, if not betrayed outright. Rather than search for new and better endings to romantic hopes for revolution or social justice, it may be more apt to ask different questions about the past. In Scott's eloquent phrasing, "to my mind thinking through the dead-end present we live in requires less a story of what we have been excluded from than a story of our desire for *that* inclusion."[8] I intend to ask how the romance of technology might be put into conversation with Scott's critique.

The challenge is twofold. The first part entails uncovering and analyzing some of those romantic narratives about technology, along with considering the ways individuals inserted themselves into these stories at the time. Histories of sound often center on listeners and producers—those who acted on or were affected by sound. Here, I will instead examine "tinkerers," or technicians with the knowledge necessary to maintain, repair, and work the machines that reproduced and delivered sound. By extension, they could also stop sonic equipment from working if they so desired. As electronically transmitted sound became more ubiquitous, it expanded repertoires of contention and of control.[9] The tinkerers were positioned to take advantage of this new configuration, as they harbored the knowledge and skills to turn up the sound or turn it off.

By placing technology and its caretakers at the center of analysis, I suggest that histories of politics must attend to the politics of sound, giving the telephone, the telegraph, and the radio the attention they received at the time. I will also reflect on the nature of the romance with technology as it played out in various scenarios. Thinking about how a variety of actors inserted themselves into the romantic narratives may offer some insight as to why they behaved as they did. What follows are three stories set in Santiago de Cuba during the 1930s and 1940s about ways in which tinkerers and law enforcement officials lent meanings to technology as they engaged in political conflicts. In the first story, technicians produced sound as subversion. In the second, repairmen cut off the sound and imagined themselves to be supporting claims for social justice. In the third, fears of espionage spurred a futile pursuit of radio pirates.

The second challenge is to avoid replicating a romance in my own narrative. Considering alternative interpretations will suggest the ways in which these were not necessarily stories of unified triumph over domination but rather of irony and fragmentation. My aim will be to offer alternative narratives of failure, complicity, or indeterminacy. More importantly,

I will try to ask new questions: How did reliance on the telephone, tele-graph, and radio shift the power dynamics among the actors involved? To what extent did the use of sonic technologies become indispensable, rather than something to be chosen or eschewed? I suggest that the promise of freedom through media such as broadcasting also became the premise for greater surveillance as law enforcement realized that new capacities meant new vulnerabilities as well.

A Culture of Tinkerers

Communications networks have historically followed capitalist in-terests. In the Caribbean, this was particularly true. The International Ocean Telegraph Company, which was formed in 1866, took the lead in connecting Cuba and the Caribbean to its system of telegraph cables. By 1870, Santiago was part of a circuit that ranged from Key West, to Cuba, Jamaica, Puerto Rico, Venezuela, and the Eastern Antilles. As U.S. and British investments and enterprises expanded throughout the Caribbean, they required the kinds of information flows that could be provided by a telegraph system. Up-to-date price quotes, weather predictions, or ship-ping times could expedite business dealings considerably. Moreover, cable companies themselves saw opportunities in the Caribbean to be the first to install these networks and therefore establish a monopoly of control over communications.[10] In addition, Cuba had a telephone system that had been installed relatively early and covered the major cities of the island.[11] Broadcasting also began early in Cuba, starting in 1922 and spreading rap-idly across the island. Because the principal medium for broadcasting at the time were telephone cables, the Cuban Telephone Company built the first broadcasting station and came to own several nationwide.[12]

The social histories of these introductions remain to be told. To begin, they must have generated a demand for people with the technical knowl-edge and skills to operate communications equipment. Telegraph and tele-phone systems needed both personnel to operate them and repair people to maintain and fix them. In this case, technology did not replace human workers as much as create a need for new kinds of workers. These technolo-gies thus fostered something of an employment boom for individuals with new specialized skills. Men (and they were mostly men) might acquire their technical capacity on their own, as they built shortwave, or "ham," radios for their own use. Tinkerers, who to this point may have concentrated their skills in hobby or leisure activities, found a market in which their capacities were valuable.[13]

Students of early radio have represented tinkerers and radio amateurs as young boys in search of amusement or middle-class hobbyists who used radio to escape from their families and chat with other amateurs in the safety of their basements.[14] In some contexts, however, these practices and skills could become highly politicized. In the Caribbean, many tinkerers and amateurs were hobbyists who spent most of their time in harmless communication with one another or with distant places, although since the equipment was difficult to acquire and expensive, there were relatively fewer men around who could be labeled "tinkerers." By the same token, the technologies that were implemented initially were transformative but not particularly widespread or densely installed. Those with specialized knowledge may have been a relatively small fraction of workers. They could, and did, use their skills to act in deliberately political ways, inserting themselves into political battles with novel strategies. These would vary with specific circumstances. Some technicians might use sabotage to silence extant networks as a way to cause trouble for governments or corporations; others would use their capacity to control and disseminate sound as a way to mobilize oppositional forces.

The Talkative Equipment

Let me begin in the 1940s with *Paginas de ayer,* a text that looks back to events in the 1930s. Juan Maria Ravelo uses the tropes of romanticism to tell a story about a clandestine radio station.[15] This station operated around the time that President Machado's regime was barely surviving on shreds of its former legitimacy. Although Gerardo Machado had been very popular among nationalists and advocates for reform when he was initially elected in 1924, the populace had largely turned against him by 1933. A hastily rewritten constitution that guaranteed his reelection in 1928 had set off a round of protests and antigovernment mobilization. The Great Depression, which hit Cuba as hard as anywhere, stripped him of any remaining domestic support. As the spring and summer of 1933 wore on and the strikes continued, the United States sent envoys and representatives to protect their considerable investments and express their increasing doubts about Machado's regime.[16]

It was in this context of "constant struggle, and desperate efforts by enemies of the regime" that the clandestine radio station began to operate in Santiago. The station was a character in a tale of political redemption: "the city listened anxiously at regular intervals, in the safety of their homes and at a prudent, low volume, to news broadcasts from a mysterious station, which struggled against the state of things . . . and spoke in the name of the revolutionaries." Not only did the station "lift the spirits of friendly ears" as the author points out, it also drove the authorities to distraction as they turned the city upside down looking for it.[17]

The heroic station did not, of course, act alone. It had an accomplice: Polanco, the radio technician who had built the very small, portable transmitter. Together, the story goes, they engaged in struggle. The intrigue began when Polanco shared his accomplishment with a friend, who happened to be a member of an anti-Machado organization. The station was then conscripted into efforts to bring down the government, despite considerable obstacles. In order to begin broadcasting, the station needed to be housed in a safe location, which proved challenging in the prevailing atmosphere of heightened suspicion and surveillance. Activists confronted rumors that all radio stations were subject to arbitrary and imminent searches, as well as the challenge of finding secure transport for the secret equipment in the middle of a transportation strike.

The narrative then reveals the way in which the station and its technicians found ways around these obstacles. They find a physician friend who is willing to use his vehicle, one of few on the road, for transport. As they are ferrying it to its new home, they nearly collide with policemen in the street. The station itself, hidden in a sack, is almost mistaken for a bag of stolen goods. The station arrives safely at the home of one of the anti-Machado associates and begins its punctual broadcasts, which both fire up the populace and infuriate law enforcement officials. In order to protect the station, the technicians spend the night with it in the house; the next day, after hearing that all radio stations are being searched and Polanco has been named as a wanted man, they decide to move it to a safer place. They move it to a house next door that had been partially destroyed by the most recent hurricane and put it in a small room where "the tiny, talkative equipment continued to be the object of intense public interest." No better place, according to Ravelo, than a ruin from which to broadcast. "The station continued its unwavering work, daring its persecutors to come after it, and coming to own the space." It transmitted not just words but also "ideas, with their undeniable power" that "expanded into the rarified space" and finally "came to forecast and predict their ultimate triumph." The narrative ends with the radio continuing its broadcasts even after Machado's downfall the following day, urging residents to act in a cordial and orderly fashion.[18]

This romance of radio seems a logical extension of and a political counterpart to the newspaper columnist who, a decade earlier, had sung easy praise and offered predictions of technology's capacity to unify and educate the multitude. This station could bring revolution to the people, inexorably and safely. Indeed, its reach overtook that of the printed word, by speaking to those who could not read or possess a newspaper. Moreover, the ephemeral nature of radio worked to its advantage. Broadcasts could be heard by anyone within range, but they left no trace. A silent receiver appeared innocent, leaving nothing tangible for authorities to hold as evidence. Like a romantic hero who "embodies the forward historical movement and drives the narrative out of the dark and into the light," the station played a leading role in the drama of revolution.[19] The narrative pronounced the 1930s as a heroic age in which technology assisted in and conspired with the struggle for social justice. Written during the 1940s in a context of messy post-Machado politics, Ravelo's narrative looks back to a simpler time. In a moment of ambiguity and compromised politics, a clear story line about the triumph of popular mobilization would have appealed to many.

Ravelo's tale of political redemption is one way to tell this story. However, even in his telling, it contains elements that spill over the constraints of a romantic narrative and open up the interpretive terrain. First, it may be relevant to note that law enforcement pursued the clandestine radio with insistence and did everything in its power to shut off the sound. If they also ascribed to a technoromance about the power of sound, one of the unintended consequences was heightened surveillance and attention to communications networks as possibly subversive. Another strand of the story worth drawing out is the complicated position of the tinkerer-cum-broadcaster. Both Polanco and the anti-Machado mobilization needed the infrastructure in place, as well as the network of radio receivers throughout the city. Moreover, he relied on the conventions elaborated as part of the practice of radio broadcasting. Commercial radio had invented those practices, including broadcasts at regular intervals and a format in which an announcer delivered news and commentary with compelling oratory, in order to attract both advertising and consumer-listeners. Indeed, the

very forces against which many anti-Machado groups were protesting—
imperialism and an overly cozy relationship with U.S. capital—were those
that had introduced radio in the first place, along with training for technicians and receivers for listeners. Scott's notion of the "desire for inclusion" is as much at work here as subversive intentions.[20] Sonic technologies
proved intrinsic to both desire and intentions.

Strikes and Sabotage

The year 1933 was a period of high levels of activism and popular expressions of discontent. Radio came to be included in the repertoire of
contention. Civil unrest and labor discontent did not end with the over-
throw of Machado; rather, they grew as the government that replaced him
seemed increasingly unsatisfactory to many Cubans. In March 1934, labor
strikes swept across the island as a broad array of workers walked off the
job. Initiated by sugar workers, the strike soon encompassed railroad and
port workers, pharmacists, bakers, food wholesalers, truckers, and shoe-
makers. The lack of essential services brought the government to the nego-
tiating table, but in the end, talks deteriorated and each side retreated. The
president suspended constitutional guarantees, a measure that included
censorship of newspapers, telegraph, and telephone lines.[21]

If the government understood how crucial the circulation of information was in this labor struggle, then so did participants. The following day,
all telephone workers from the Cuban Telephone Company walked away
from their jobs. Many of them also cut cables on their way out, debilitating
the network for at least ten days. This move silenced 33,000 telephones in
Havana and 6,000 in the provincial areas. In addition, six radio stations
and the wires dedicated to transmitting banking and financial information, also controlled by the Cuban Telephone Company, fell silent.[22] As
the strike dragged on, food rotted on docks and the government tried to
silence its critics, including newspapers. However, it had more difficulty
coping with the silent telephones. Because their actions had such disruptive consequences, telephone workers were, according to the newspapers,
among the strikers the government found the most difficult to deal with.[23]
For some of those employees of the telephone company, the government
reserved an extreme reaction. Twenty were arrested and forced to work at
gunpoint.[24] Four days later, the government had managed to find enough
strikebreakers to get the telephone service running again. When they

could not find people willing to work the telephones, they used members of the military and Rural Guard, but these new workers must have faced considerable challenges. Strikers inflicted at least $100,000 in damage through sabotage of the equipment, and the recently hired may or may not have been sufficiently trained to use and repair it.[25]

In this context, a repairman could wield a great deal of power. The documentary record has left a few traces of the ways tinkerers were able to disrupt the flow of communication and, in some instances, unsettle the certainties of those purportedly in control. For example, the *Tribunal de Urgencia* in Santiago heard a number of cases arising from conflicts between the replacements and the strikers or their associates. In the midst of the March strike, José Maria Blanco, a thirty-year-old repairman from Spain, was accused by rural guardsman Armelio Sierra of cutting all the telephone lines in Holguín and stealing all the tools from the main telephone office, effectively cutting off communication by telephone. Sierra also maintained that Blanco had taken many coils needed to make the phones work, leaving only the ones for the barracks, city hall, hospital, fire station, and pharmacy. The judge ordered the female telephone workers to testify. Of the five women who testified, only one saw him take coils, but she asserted that he did not take any tools. None testified that he had cut any wires. When Blanco himself testified, he admitted to taking the coils in order to support striking workers, but he denied cutting wires or stealing tools. He returned the coils and replaced them one week later, thus restoring service.[26]

This episode raises a few questions. The rural guardsman who had been placed in a supervisory role revealed that he had a vague grasp of the machines in question. Had he asserted that the wires were cut in order to inflate the charges or to defend his own inability to replace the missing coils? Was Blanco the only repairman in the area, and were those the only coils available? The documents do not answer these questions, but it is possible to surmise that Blanco's ability to cause such a serious crisis speaks both to the increasingly important role of telephone communications in 1930s Cuba and to the way that those with a measure of technical knowledge could intervene in labor conflicts and exert some influence. The Rural Guard's belief in the indispensable nature of transmitted sound and his ignorance of the workings of the telephone led him to exaggerate Blanco's actions. If the advent of technologies meant greater surveillance, then it also resulted in bungled prosecutions. Blanco himself seemed to be acting within an understanding, in this case quite accurate, that he could control and disrupt major communications networks.

In July 1934, the Cuban Telephone Company workers struck again in a dispute about how the initial strike had been settled.[27] More than one thousand workers pulled all the fuses in the central office and cut out all lines to the United States. Again, this disrupted communications on the island as well as between banks and stockbrokers. Newspapers used words such as *paralyzed* to describe the state of the island. Two weeks later, the ongoing strike led the government to a drastic measure. It took over the U.S. owned Cuban Telephone Company, prompting worries in the United States that this might be the beginning of a trend threatening numerous U.S. investments in Cuba. In any case, additional anxiety about the possibility of sabotage also resulted in the reinforcement of military guards at the telephone offices.[28]

Labor escalated the conflict on August 12 as the telegraph and mail workers joined the strike to mark the anniversary of Machado's downfall. The sense of crisis heightened as the Cuban army proved incapable of delivering the mail. As the newspapers reported, the only way to communicate any information was through the few independent broadcasting stations whose personnel were not on strike. Still, conveying personal messages through radio broadcasts was undoubtedly an unsatisfying and inefficient way of proceeding.[29] Even if the military had succeeded in their efforts to replace all striking workers, they had to cope with damaged and missing equipment. The army and navy communications services were barely adequate to cover crucial government dispatches but not much else. Under heavy military guard, undertrained replacements scrambled to cover at least some hobbled telegraph, telephone, and mail services.

It was in this context that any sign of trouble was used as an excuse to invoke sabotage and clamp down on strikers, as government officials panicked in the face of technology's failure. The same day that telegraph workers resumed their strike, José Antonio Pascual, an employee of the Santiago telegraph office, was turned in by his acting supervisor. The man complained that Pascual had refused to go to the train station to pick up shipments (literally suitcases full) of telegrams, which were arriving in this unusual manner because of the strike. Pascual acknowledged that he had indeed refused, but he pointed out that since it had been a Sunday, there would have been no delivery. Since there was no real charge, Pascual was released on the following day, August 14.[30] For some reason, however, the judge was dissatisfied and pursued the case further by ordering that a telegram asking for more information on the case be sent to a judge in a different district. Unfortunately, because of the strike, this request did not arrive in the neighboring town until August 20. Pascual again appeared before a judge on August 23, but by that time, a general amnesty for striking workers had been declared, and the case was dropped.[31]

The details of the case suggest that the supervisor, a member of the Rural Guard, was unfamiliar with the workings of the office and quick to accuse this particular worker of a misdemeanor—an accusation that revealed his lack of leverage in demanding that workers do as they were ordered. It also reminds us of the real disruption of the court system that was possible if communications workers struck. The small example of such a long delay in a relatively trivial case underscores the crucial nature of these technologies at that time. If among the telegrams that went undelivered were those from courts and judges attempting to try the very people responsible for the disruption, technology, or lack thereof, trumped and thwarted the law. Nevertheless, once the strikers went back to work, they would also necessarily be serving not only their immediate supervisors but also all branches of government, including the court system and law enforcement officials.

In some cases, fear of sabotage guided fitful reactions. During the same week that Pascual was arrested, Angel Báez, a twenty-one-year-old unemployed telegraph worker was also picked up and accused of stealing three plugs from the telegraph office in Holguín, a town near Santiago. Without the plugs, there was no service. The Rural Guard responded rather ineffectively. Initially, they spent a day in fruitless pursuit of Báez and the plugs. It was only the following day that they decided to search the office and find new plugs to substitute for the stolen ones. The accused denied any wrongdoing, and before his case could get too far, he was released under a declaration of amnesty. This minor incident reveals the disjuncture between the actual threat and the perceived threat. Because he was acknowledged to have "knowledge of telegraphy," Báez managed to raise the suspicions of the authorities and silence the telegraph office for an entire day. If what he wanted was to disorient and befuddle the Rural Guard, substituting for telegraph workers, then he succeeded.[32]

In this drama of labor dissent and the subversion of order, knowledge mattered, and it enabled an unemployed twenty-one-year-old to get the best of systems of control. It was the very power of the suggestion that technology, or knowledge of it, could be subversive that ultimately led to heightened suspicion and greater vigilance. At the same time, the combination of vigilance and ignorance only led to inept law enforcement. This story privileges neither workers' triumph nor state domination; rather, it reveals the uneven stumbles and misapprehensions through which these media acquired meaning.

In the above episodes, sound, or the absence of it, indicated a great deal about the faltering control of the state when confronted by more knowledgeable technicians. The power wielded by technical ability, though, is largely negative in these stories: the strikers or repairmen cut off service, stopping flows of information and interpersonal, commercial, or government communications. In other instances, tinkerers found ways to further harness the power of sound. Rather than silence, tinkerers got into trouble by making noise or by merely being suspected of so doing. A much more drawn out drama of espionage and clandestine radios speaks to the ongoing conflicts and continuing romances that underwrote sonic technologies.[33] In this case, both accusers and accused made meaning of shortwave broadcasting through tropes of heroism and authority.

War and Radio Spies

By World War II, radio amateurs, rather than repairmen or workers, fell under suspicion of subversion. Since shortwave transmitters and receivers were considerably more complex than telegraph or telephone equipment, authorities often found them utterly mystifying. Stories of espionage and xenophobia along with vague knowledge about the technicalities of wireless communications gave rise to accusation and reprisal.

On October 3, 1941, Domingo Gordin, a firefighter living in Santiago, was arrested on grounds that he was using his amateur radio equipment to conduct communications with fascist sympathizers in foreign countries. Prompted by a police accusation, a court official entered and searched his house. Two experts accompanied him: the radio inspector for the region, Rafael Miranda Sablón, and a sergeant from the Cuban Army's Signal Corps, who would presumably assist in recognizing equipment capable of the alleged transmissions. Once they completed their search of Gordin's house and equipment, the court official declared that they had found and seized a 50-watt transmitter that was "ready to communicate with foreign countries."[34]

Gordin's lawyer submitted a defense stating that the station was licensed and therefore legal and claiming that Gordin neither knew foreign languages nor was a Nazi sympathizer. He also dismissed the notion that there might be military secrets to communicate from Santiago. In any case, he argued, any untoward communication would have been intercepted either by the Americans or by nearby islands that were part of the British Empire, and there was no record at all of any such activity. Gordin also submitted a statement claiming that he had a license and only used the station to communicate with other radio aficionados in Cuba.

Acosta, the police chief whose suspicions led to Gordin's arrest, was acting on a notion of technology as a powerfully unifying force (albeit for unsavory purposes). In this case, the danger lay not in interrupted communication; to the contrary, it lurked with the suggestion of clandestine exchanges with perceived enemies. The possibility of secret sounds traversing long distances between two parties engaged in illicit transfers of information was enough to warrant an arrest. That the investigator brought two so-called experts with him speaks to their assumptions about the central role of the equipment itself to his accusation. It also speaks to his inability to discern whether the equipment was indeed "dangerous." Gordin and his lawyer did not try to deny the importance of the equipment. Instead, they merely tried to disprove the accusation of Gordin's participation in illicit practices. Ironically, his radio was not in fact powerful enough to communicate with foreign countries, but the presumed experts somehow missed this and supported Acosta's statement.

Meanwhile, Acosta ordered a second person arrested, a German named Rodolfo Stohl. He seemed to pose a much greater threat, since the remainder of the case file focuses mostly on his past and background. Stohl was a radio engineer who arrived in Cuba in 1928, found work at a Philips store in Havana, and then ended up in Santiago, where, pretending to be Dutch, he opened a radio repair shop. The documentation is not very clear on Stohl's whereabouts when the war broke out. He attested to traveling to Havana, losing his passport and identification card, and then returning to Santiago. Both the police and Stohl himself asserted that he had befriended radio amateurs as well as the director of the radio station CMQ in Santiago. The court requested several investigations of Stohl, and although they are somewhat contradictory, they all agree that he was a very skilled radio repairman and operator.

With that assertion, those who seem to be intent on convicting him built rumors and allegations. The Santiago police, including Acosta and his lieutenant Rosales, claimed to have amassed certain evidence that he was involved in spying and other nefarious activities. When Stohl had returned to Santiago, they argued, he had appeared at a local radio station and boasted about plans to build two stations, forty kilometers apart, with another German friend. He had, according to Acosta, passed around pictures of himself in a German army uniform. Moreover, he had asked to spend the night at the station, claiming that he did not have anywhere else to go. The director testified that he had feared Stohl would use his considerable skills to convert the equipment from longwave to shortwave in the middle of the night and engage in illicit communications with foreign countries.

These elements together rendered Stohl a dubious character: he was German, he knew a lot about radio, and he was a vagrant—a rather gregarious one whose acquaintances were vulnerable to conversion to treacherous activities. All these qualities, following the police logic, added up to a very suspicious type: the clandestine radio spy. Stohl met the requirements to play a part in a technodystopia of treason and betrayal. They arrested him and tried to build a case against both Stohl and Gordin, accusing them of sharing an intention to communicate with enemy nations.

After Stohl's arrest, the court requested testimony from a number of other investigators, including José Portuondo, an agent with the secret police, and Jaime Roldos Arche, a special investigator from the judicial police in Havana. With Rosales of the Santiago police insisting on his accusations that both men were involved in espionage and communications with Nazi sympathizers, the two specialists refuted these allegations. Portuondo claimed that the station was properly licensed; that Gordin was not a Nazi sympathizer; and, most importantly, that the equipment was not in fact powerful enough to send or receive messages from foreign countries. Roldos, more focused on Stohl, listed numerous arrests and convictions for robbery and vandalism. He agreed that Stohl had a great deal of technical ability, but he emphatically denied any involvement in espionage activities with Gordin or anyone else. In the end, the defense of Gordin rested on two main points: that he was a man of "scanty intelligence" with no knowledge of foreign languages and, more importantly, that his equipment could not possibly communicate with foreign countries. One wonders why it took so much testimony and so many experts to establish this key point. Most of the authorities were at a disadvantage, it seemed, because they themselves were unable to verify whether their suspects had the proper training and whether the equipment could do what they suspected. Both men were released from jail once it became evident that the case rested on flimsy foundations and more anxiety than information.

The accusers, witnesses, and law enforcement personnel shared a story about sound as a protagonist in a tale of subversion. They imagined the tinkerers Stohl and Gordin thinking of themselves as participants in a larger story and fighting for a cause. That the cause was reprehensible to them did not change the romantic overtones. The police fashioned a narrative with an embattled hero and a marvelous machine that could wreak a lot of havoc. Gordin himself, who did not take part in this narrative, was caught unsuspecting in a tale spun by others. In this instance, the romance of radio supported stepped-up suspicion and surveillance, but it did not yield a clear triumph. Since the case depended on knowledge, when that knowledge was lacking, it fell apart. No longer actors conforming to a script, Gordin may have resumed his amateur radio activites and Stohl likely continued to roam, stealing here and fixing radios there, while the police were left to search for another victim with whom they might earn the approval of their superiors in the campaign against Nazi sympathizers and spies.

All three of these stories share a relationship to the romance of the subversive capacity of technology. In some cases, however, although the drama began with all the elements in place, it did not unfold according to a romantic script. Although Arevalo placed the clandestine radio and its operator into a seamless narrative of communication as revolution, the documentary record bears evidence of messier outcomes. Striking workers may have been inserting themselves into a double romance of embattled labor and the power of technology, which was shared by those who intended to stop them. However, the stories fizzle out in the face of uncertainty or evasion rather than clear triumph or failure. Nevertheless, they all indicate an increased vulnerability brought on by a reliance on machines that convey information. This cut both ways: workers or strikers could be brought down by effective control of communications by the state, as when it imposed censorship or surveillance of telephone lines, but the state could just as easily lose control of a situation absent the same tools of communication. In the episode involving Gordin and Stohl, the romance of subversive technology proved a powerful impetus in the hands of law enforcement—more so than in the heads of the hapless Gordin or the skilled but seemingly aimless Stohl. The disparity in intention meant that the actors were playing parts in different dramas: if the Santiago police had an idea that they might heroically thwart attempts at espionage, Gordin and Stohl seemed to be, from the evidence, characters in a picaresque novel.

If we revisit the questions posed at the beginning of this chapter, some reflections are in order. The presence of technology shifted power dynamics in several ways. First, it prompted the emergence of the tinkerer as a player in political life. Someone with technical knowledge could put that knowledge to work in the service of an ideal of their choosing. Mere employees, who in other contexts did not have much leverage, might now hold their companies or an entire city hostage if they so desired. By the same token, radio technicians who developed a political agenda or were drafted into a movement might pose a much greater threat to their perceived enemies than ever before. Power emanated not from a monopoly on legitimate violence or from the mobilized "masses" but from access to and, importantly, knowledge of machines that could talk. This suggests the need to rethink models of power that depend on "top-down" or popular notions of political change. Taking technology into account means conceiving of a reorganized political space in which access to either force or popular support may not tell the whole story. This is a complicated history. The advent of tinkerers who posed a threat may mean heightened surveillance, but it may also mean flawed and faltering surveillance, rather than an easy harnessing of technology. To the contrary, in the end, what grew was perhaps the dependence on technology and the vulnerability that accompanied it. Technology made sound a weapon in political struggles, and some wielded it more deftly than others. Nevertheless, it became part of the story—a factor that was indispensable to all participants who were no longer able to imagine proceeding without sonic technologies. Even as their conflicts escalated, violently opposed groups came to share assumptions about the advantages of having a tinkerer on their side.

5

MUSIC, MEDIA SPECTACLE, AND THE IDEA OF DEMOCRACY

The Case of DJ Kermit's "Góber"

Alejandro L. Madrid

ON FEBRUARY 14, 2006, the Mexican newspaper *La Jornada* and W Radio published and broadcast a telephone conversation between Mario Marín, the governor of the state of Puebla, and Kamel Nacif, an influential Puebla-based businessman linked to international child pornography and prostitution networks. The recording confirmed the complicity of the governor in kidnapping and trying to imprison Lydia Cacho, a journalist who a few months earlier had made public Nacif's pedophilia connections in her book *Los demonios del Edén.*[1] The conversation, charged with profanity and crude misogynist language, was played ad nauseam on television and radio over the next couple of weeks, making it an integral part of the Mexican soundscape and igniting a media frenzy that quickly came to be known as the *góber precioso* (precious governor) affair. The event displayed practices of corruption, misogyny, and censorship pervading Mexico's political life, and it was tacitly presented as an exercise in journalistic independence and the "newly conquered" democratic right to question the government— arguably, a right won by Mexican television networks with the election of

71

a democratic government in 2000 that allowed breaking the hegemony of the National Revolutionary Party (PRI) and its caudillo-worshiping culture.[2] As such, the invasion of the Mexican soundscape by the voices of el góber precioso and Kamel Nacif reverberated with the rhetorical use of the concept of democracy that the new government had persistently celebrated since taking over the Mexican presidency. It seemed that finally, as a result of this new democracy, censorship was over and the media were able to publicly criticize the government. However, in this chapter, I argue that the development of the góber precioso affair itself was a signal of how the very concept of democracy had been eroded, becoming meaningless due to its indiscriminate and almost cynical presence in the Mexican public sphere.

A little over a week after the infamous recording was first broadcast, Mexico City native Francisco Reyes—"DJ Kermit"—produced "Góber (Precioso)," an electronic dance music (EDM) track based on samples taken from the conversation.[3] "Góber" came out right in the middle of the media frenzy and was immediately praised by journalist Luis Felipe Castañeda as the next "Macarena," a track that would "surely become the most requested [single] at dance events in Mexico."[4] Indeed, within a week, the track entered the top ten list of most discotheques, clubs, radio stations, and music critics in central Mexico. In *Memorias de una infamia*, a comprehensive story of the pedophile case that triggered her arrest, Lydia Cacho acknowledges DJ Kermit's track as part of an almost parodist process where "the 'góber precioso' songs are danced to at trendy discotheques, there are Internet videogames, and the terrible original calls between Nacif and Marín were sold as cellular phone ringtones."[5] According to Cacho, this is an example of "the supine Mexican ability to trivialize major problems like this, like corruption, is what strengthens the dehumanization, the lack of compassion, and the mediocrity in which the country is immersed. Eventually everything becomes a joke, a gag, it is normalized, it is disqualified, it dissolves in the lack of desire to transform ourselves."[6]

Although I agree that DJ Kermit's track somehow manages to hit a humorous chord within the reception of an otherwise horrendous event, I differ with Cacho's interpretation that it trivializes it. Instead, I argue that a close study of both the track as a sound text and its place within the larger góber precioso affair sheds light upon a number of cultural processes that range from the use of humor to make visible, criticize, and deal with painful corruption practices to the way that media co-opts a concept such as democracy and transforms it into a consumption good through marketing strategies. In the context of the transformation of DJ to music producer, "Góber" challenges the stereotype of EDM as pure hedonistic pleasure and illuminates a current shift in DJ cultures: the articulation of local politics and media by a global music trend.[7] What are the local particularities expressed in the global EDM style of "Góber"? How do the processes of production and distribution of "Góber" reflect the simulacrum-like character (its status as representation passing as reality) of the media spectacle generated by the góber precioso affair? How do the local particularities at stake in "Góber" as a Mexican phenomenon inform our understanding of global networks such as the music industry and globally circulating ideas like democracy? By tackling these questions, this chapter seeks to find out how listening practices can inform an understanding of the social processes as well as political and cultural fabric that enables, nurtures, and provides them with local meaning. Taking into account Cacho's concerns, problematizing and expanding on them through Guy Debord's notion of "spectacle" as "a view of the world that has become objective [and which language of signs is] at the same time the ultimate end product of that system,"[8] I explore the complex processes of representation of the góber precioso affair and the processes of production and distribution of DJ Kermit's "Góber" as they are mediated by the paradoxical ways in which rating-based media displays are constructed into façades of democracy. By using interviews and archival evidence vis-à-vis a discussion of musical style, I seek to offer a cultural critique of the track, the music industry, and the media's use of music as part of larger processes of commodification. This chapter shows that the ironic sense of humor in DJ Kermit's track is both a commentary on the growing rejection, disappointment, and lack of respect that Mexican upper-middle classes feel toward the ruling elites of their country and evidence of the fear that the absolute power of government still arouses in citizens. I argue that, when read within the specific historical circumstances that surrounded it, the affair shows a new balance of power and the shifting ground upon which a new type of collaboration between media and government was negotiated. Furthermore, the situation puts in evidence the media's commodification of ideas such as "democracy" and "freedom of speech" under Mexico's post-2000 neoliberal rule. Indeed, the contradictory reaction of the media a few months after the events took place, the passing of the Ley Federal de Radio y Televisión (Federal Radio and Television Law) by Congress shortly before the 2006 presidential election,[9] and the one-sided media coverage of that campaign (when the candidate of the party in power received privileged coverage while the opposition candidates were systematically criticized and often slandered) suggests that the góber precioso affair was instead a façade of democracy—a spectacle that responded more to media ratings than to a real attempt to systematically question corrupt practices within the Mexican political system.

Spectacle and the Góber Precioso Affair

In 2005, Mexican journalist and human-rights activist Lydia Cacho published *Los demonios del Edén*. The book was the result of years of interest in the phenomenon of trafficking women for prostitution and in sexual abuse cases in the southeastern Mexican city of Cancún. In the book, Cacho publishes interviews with alleged child-sexual-abuse victims of businessman Jean Succar Kuri (at the time, he was under arrest in Arizona for child pornography), and it accuses textile tycoon Kamel Nacif of trying to protect Kuri and his child prostitution ring. Nacif's response was to charge Cacho with defamation in a Puebla state court. Eight months after the book was published, on December 16, 2005, a Puebla police group crossed state lines to illegally "arrest" Cacho outside of her office in Cancún, Quintana Roo.[10] After a twenty-hour car trip, during which she was threatened and psychologically tortured, the journalist was imprisoned in Puebla.[11] Due to pressure from international civil right activists and nongovernmental organizations, Cacho was soon released from jail after paying a USD $6,500 bail but not without being further harassed and denied a lawyer and doctor while in prison. The crime with which Cacho was charged was a misdemeanor that did not merit jail time, not to mention the fact that the Puebla police had no authority to arrest someone in another state. Clearly, in order for these actions to take place, a number of concerted (some might say corrupted) efforts from authorities in both Puebla and Quintana Roo were necessary, including the will of someone powerful enough behind the operation to be able to mobilize these actions.

The publicized telephone conversation—which took place sometime around December 19, shortly after Cacho's kidnapping—revealed Nacif thanking Puebla governor Mario Marín for his help in "punishing" Cacho, and it eventually put in evidence the active role of the governor in this illicit affair. As mentioned earlier, the conversation was first made public by the nationwide leftist newspaper *La Jornada*; this early dissemination was followed by its pervasive presence in Televisa and TV Azteca, the two national television networks, as well as local and nationwide radio shows and printed media. As a result of such bombardment, the voices of Marín and Nacif—as well as the infamous góber precioso salute—became recognizable elements in the Mexican cultural soundscape. In addition to the uproar ignited by the incriminating nature of the conversation, the obvious foul language and the sexual and homoerotic innuendos that permeate it helped to make the repeated media performance of the recording into a hyped media show.

Like the media frenzy surrounding the góber precioso affair, "Góber" would seem to be an exercise in artistic freedom of expression—an instance when a creative local musician used his craft and humor to denounce extended practices of corruption. However, a closer scrutiny of its processes of production and distribution reveals it as a more complex site where mainstream and underground marketing issues and strategies intersect and reveal a more ambiguous relation toward the event that inspired it and the media frenzy that fueled it. In fact, "Góber" did not come about solely as DJ Kermit's reaction against the horrifying corruption practices exposed by the góber precioso affair or the Mexican audience's ability to ridicule the protagonists of the affair. Instead, the idea to produce the track came from an informal chat with Jaime Almeida, an influential music journalist and radio and television host who was already familiar with Kermit's early track "I Have a Dream," which sampled from Martin Luther King Jr.'s historical speech. DJ Kermit explains, "Two days before I made the track I received the Best DJ/Producer prize from the DJ & Clubbing Awards. After the ceremony, Jaime Almeida, the president of the jury, told me, 'Hey! I heard your track "I Have a Dream" and liked it a lot. . . . Why don't you produce something else based on a political topic?' There was a big fuss about the góber precioso phone call, so as a joke I told him, 'OK, I'll do one for the Góber.' And he said, 'Really? Make it and I'll play it on the radio right away.'"[12] DJ Kermit finished the track after a couple of days and brought it to Almeida's office at Mexico City's Radio Fórmula as promised. Almeida immediately called Ciro Gómez Leyva, the station's leading anchorman (whose daily news show was about to begin) and assured him he had a "musical bomb" for his program. Word of Almeida's musical finding quickly spread throughout the radio station, and a sizeable crowd gathered at Gómez Leyva's office waiting to hear Almeida's latest discovery. Only one minute and fifteen seconds into the track, when the sampled voice of Kamel Nacif came out of the loudspeakers stating "¿Que pasó mi góber precioso?" (What's happened, my precious governor?), was the attentive silence of the audience replaced by loud collective laughter. Needless to say, DJ Kermit's "Góber" premiered without delay on Gómez Leyva's highly rated show.

Clearly, the composition of "Góber," the excitement about its release, and its early dissemination owe much to the mainstream media and its rating-motivated marketing approach. It was because the recorded conversation was already a ubiquitous presence in Mexican sonic life due to its continuous media repetition that made it an appealing and even amusing subject for music. Moreover, the distribution plan followed by DJ Kermit soon after reveals one of the most interesting glocal aspects of current EDM: the intersection of mainstream and underground marketing strategies. After it had been played on Gómez Leyva's radio show and labeled by the nationally circulating newspaper *Reforma* as the "next 'Macarena,'"[13] DJ Kermit made the track available as a free download for three days and sent the link to his list of contacts. Internet sites hosting the track soon proliferated, and many music and political chat rooms, blogs, and listservs made it a topic of discussion. It was a few days later when DJ Kermit walked into Mexico City's Tasqueña subway station and was offered a pirate copy of his own track that he realized the type of underground phenomenon that "Góber" had become. This became clear when, about a month after its media premiere, the newspaper *Reforma* actually suggested that the track was more requested than those by many well-known pop singers: "Musical hits like RBD, Intocable, Luis Miguel, and even Alejandro Fernández went down in the Top Ten chart before the hit of the moment: 'Góber (Precioso).' Only a few days after the release of its remix version, composed by DJ Kermit, the melody made its way into piracy markets, with unexpected results for the street vendors of Puebla's capital."[14] The underground success of "Góber" should be understood not only as a direct effect of the continuous presence of the góber precioso affair in the media but also as a result of what it meant for regular citizens—the affair was the sonic confirmation of the type of corruption they had always presumed but for which had never had proof, and DJ Kermit's track was a waggish musical commentary that made its everyday presence morally bearable.

The success of the track was soon picked up by the powerful Mexican label Musart, which offered DJ Kermit a five-year contract for the exclusive rights of the track and its commercial distribution in the United States. Convinced that Musart's deal was an excellent opportunity to advance his career, Kermit accepted the offer. However, it would be a decision he would soon regret.

> I gave them freedom to do versions of the track . . . and they made five versions for the CD, including *reggaeton*, *grupera*, and *pasito duranguense*. They were made by Musart musicians, and they were really bad. It was truly awful. I kept asking them not to release it like that, but they didn't care, they said it was an urgent matter since the topic was hot. Furthermore, they said they couldn't use the original voice of Kamel Nacif and used instead an imitator. For me the whole thing was a big disappointment. Indeed, for the kind of change [in my career] I was looking for it didn't help at all that ["Góber"] came out as *pasito duranguense*.[15]

The reason for DJ Kermit's disappointment with Musart was a conflict of representations and desires. Musart's production of reggaeton, *cumbia*, and pasito duranguense remixes of "Góber" was a savvy marketing strategy aimed at articulating the success of these genres among the Mexican and Latino working classes. However, Musart's desire to appeal to and economically benefit from a larger working-class market clashed with DJ Kermit's desire to belong to the cosmopolitan, more sophisticated, and worldly EDM scene.

DJ Kermit's hybrid distribution process, appealing to both underground and mainstream markets, is usual among EDM producers worldwide. The increasing ubiquity of EDM is strongly connected to the producer's ability to take advantage of the new technologies of production and distribution and engage mainstream marketing strategies. Electronic and cyber technologies allow musicians and producers to work around channels of mass distribution and give power to underground strategies that infuse their product with an aura of uniqueness and prestige often absent in mainstream commercial artifacts.[16] For local EDM producers such as DJ Kermit, the ability to be recognized by the mainstream and keep their underground appeal is crucial to shape the glocal character of their musical endeavors.

In their classic essay on the "culture industry," Horkheimer and Adorno argue that under capitalism the production of culture follows the mass-producing logic of industrial manufacturing.[17] Their critique of the "culture industry" offers a vision of a society unable to cultivate true freedom and individuality. Although the logic of commodification at stake in their critique still informs the unbalanced relationship between creative individuals and the mainstream music industry, the different character of a "culture industry" that has dramatically changed since the 1940s offers a picture much more complex than the kind of alienation proposed by Horkheimer and Adorno. However, one still can find use for Adorno and Horkheimer's ideas when taking a look at how cultural artifacts such as music are used in the commodification of concepts and notions (such as democracy or freedom) that are constructed as cornerstones of Western social organization. The case of the góber precioso affair as sonic representation of practices assumed to exist but rendered invisible shows the complex ways in which media works to commodify these notions in the context of Mexican cultural life.

The story of DJ Kermit's "Góber" was, from its very beginning, one of taking advantage of a media-rate frenzy but disguised as an exercise in democracy at a critically contested political moment in the country's history. It was also a reflection on the meaning of a globally circulating idea such as democracy within the specific local circumstances of Mexican politics, Mexican media, and the Mexican public sphere. Jaime Almeida and Ciro Gómez Leyva's excitement about first broadcasting "Góber" and Musart's rushed CD production and release in order to have it ready while the topic was still "hot" can only be understood when interpreting the production of the track not as a result of the góber precioso affair but as an intrinsic part of this media spectacle. It was a spectacle that appealed to the imagination of a democratic ideal, which eventually performed a particular idea of what democracy was, looked, and sounded like, making it into an imaginary commodity for consumption. Such an exercise shows how, in a sign system such as media and media marketing, a representation (a sign system in itself) becomes the end product of that very system. In other words, in a media-based affair such as the góber precioso, what is at stake is not democracy itself but rather its representation, its simulacrum according to the very codes for the production of consumer goods that governs media itself. Such a circular dynamic only shows the emptiness of the idea of democracy at a very specific and politically contested moment in Mexican history.

At the same time, Musart's transformation of Kermit's cosmopolitan EDM music into simulacra of working-class grupero and pasito duranguense styles overpowered the DJ's attempt to link his track to the aura and prestige of the alternative via an underground distribution strategy. Musart's marketing strategy effectively appropriated the track's underground aura and made it into a mere commercial product of consumption.

DJ Kermit expands: "I made 'Góber' in a more commercial style. It is a club theme and it doesn't really fit in with the rest of my set, which is more underground, more electro and tribal. Besides after the problem with Musart I was very disappointed and decided not to play it anymore."[18] The media spectacle surrounding the track became so embedded in the Mexican popular imagination that DJ Kermit's name came to be inseparable from "Góber" even for hardcore EDM Mexican fans in ways unforeseen by the musician. In June 2007, Minerva Ocampo, a clubber and blogger from Mexico City, posted a blog describing an EDM party that featured DJ Kermit, and she felt compelled to say, "To remind you of Kermit, some dorks out there should remember a remix of the very famous conversation between the góber precioso and Succar Kuri, well, that's by Kermit."[19] Indeed, much to DJ Kermit's dismay, the success of the track made his name an intrinsic part of the affair and of an EDM style he did not want to cultivate.

Since the track became a success among middle-class clubbers and was produced by a middle-class DJ, one could also interpret the musician's disillusion with "Góber" and Musart's appropriation of the track's aura as a metaphor for the growing disappointment that Mexican upper-middle classes feel toward the ruling elites of their country and their systematic corruption of the public sphere. Clearly, the humor perceived in the track is not intrinsic to the music or the composition; rather, it emerges in its reception and in the fertile ground these very negative feelings, awoken by the unexpected presence of Nacif's voice, provide. Furthermore, I would argue that the commodification of the track and its transformation into simulacra of working-class products could also be seen as metaphors for the kind of spectacle that takes over or attempts to shape the idea of democracy through media. In both cases, the resulting spectacle is reduced to a consumer good that is nevertheless recognized by informed general audiences as a simulacrum. As such, it becomes the source of tacit rejection, as in the case of DJ Kermit's attempt to separate himself from his own track, or ridicule, as in the general reaction of laughter at the samples of the conversation.

Listening to "Góber (Precioso)"

Regardless of its willing or unwilling role in the media spectacle generated by the góber precioso affair, "Góber" is a powerful statement that reveals the disdain felt by the Mexican middle classes toward the political elite of its country. A careful exploration of the sounds in the track, as well as those that resonate loudly by virtue of their absence from the track, provides a window into the structures of feeling—the shared social and cultural codes that inform both the composition process and the listening practices generated by this music.

The musical style of the track is a type of Latin house in which synthesized sounds appear as commentaries to the sampled telephone conversation. The punctuating cow bell and the *güiro* rhythmic pattern throughout the track, the clever idea of thinning the musical texture while accompanying each conversation sample with a festive clave rhythmic pattern (which somehow emphasizes the bizarre character of the affair), and the cheerful house elements (synthesized bass and melodic lines) that follow each sample all point toward an irony that sarcastically mocks the individuals caught on tape. In "Góber," musical style works as a type of carnivalesque subversion of social hierarchy and status that under normal circumstances would be impossible.

Although the ironic sense of humor in DJ Kermit's track is a commentary on the growing rejection, disappointment, and disdain that middle classes feel toward political life in Mexico, the selection of samples reveals a different feeling toward the country's political elite. DJ Kermit selected portions of the conversation between Marín and Nacif that reminded the listener of the darkest corruption that existed between the two people. Thus, "*al señor gobernador no le tembló la mano*" (the hand of the governor didn't tremble) refers to the governor's unofficial order to arrest Lydia Cacho, drive her from Cancún to Puebla, psychologically torture her, and throw her in jail where custodians received orders to allow her to be raped.[20] The phrase "*te tengo aquí una botella bellísima de un coñac*" (I have a beautiful cognac bottle for you) allegedly refers not to the French liquor but rather to an underage girl.[21] Nevertheless, the voice of the governor is absent from the track. DJ Kermit explains his decision: "Yes, I was afraid that someone would get pissed, so forget about it! Who would want to mess with these people? So I decided not to use the voice of the governor. I mean, even without the governor's voice, *Milenio* published that Kamel Nacif was thinking about suing me, and I was like 'Crap!' But then I thought, 'How is he gonna sue me if he claims his is not the voice in the recording?'"[22] Clearly, DJ Kermit's decision to not use the voice of the governor is in line with the generalized fear among Mexicans of a political system considered perverse and corrupt. To paraphrase a popular Mexican saying, the voice of Marín *brilla por su ausencia* (shines due to its absence). Under these circumstances, the governor's silence in the track is a cry louder than his actual voice would be, and it thus becomes a phantasmatic, subliminal presence upon which popular fears, suspicions, and desires can be projected. DJ Kermit's track, with the absence of the governor's voice, shows how the musician negotiated his own fears by stripping them from the final product. However, for listeners, the absence of the governor's voice from the track plays a double role. On one hand, it renders the event easier to ridicule; on the other, it makes the governor and what he represents for listeners (the corrupt practices of the Mexican government) into a kind of specter whose presence can be felt even when not actually seen or heard.

The reception of "Góber" also offers an opportunity to further measure the Mexican public opinion toward political life. DJ Kermit recalls, "The first time I played it live, people already knew about it. In fact, I played it because they were asking for it. I took my time before playing it, and when I did, after the first sample, everyone started laughing."[23] When I went to Mexico City to conduct fieldwork, DJ Kermit had already decided to stop playing "Góber" as part of his live set. Thus, unable to witness the live reaction of dancing fans, I had to arrange sessions to play the track to randomly selected individuals who were unfamiliar with it. The reaction after hearing the first recorded sample of Nacif was invariably the same: laughter. Such reactions resonate with the amused crowd gathered outside of Gómez Leyva's office when DJ Kermit played the first copy of his demo for him and Almeida. This does not come as a surprise if we consider that even when Kermit told Almeida he was going to make the track, he thought of it as a joke ("as a joke I told him, 'OK, I'll do one for the góber'"). Such reactions clearly resonate with the ironic sense of humor found in the track's musical style. Just as DJ Kermit made the track's style into a space of symbolic critique, dancing fans made its performance on the dance floor into a similar type of subversion that reflects the structure of feelings among most Mexican citizens toward the political elites of their country.

The day after "Góber" was first broadcast, Katia D'Artígues published a column in which she states, "So, this góber precioso affair could become an industry in itself. Yesterday, Ciro Gómez Leyva and Jaime Almeida presented a song titled 'Góber.'"[24] As I have mentioned, the complex and paradoxical ways in which rating-based media spectacles are constructed into facades of democracy should be taken into account when examining the production, distribution, and reception of "Góber." D'Artígues's ironic remark reminds us of the current relevance of some aspects of Horkheimer and Adorno's classic discussion on the culture industry—particularly of issues related to the logic of commodification. Furthermore, when we analyze the góber precioso media spectacle and its tacit invocation of democracy and transparency under the light of commodification, we understand that industry and culture become interwoven in the production of modern entertainment strategies and technologies. Here, the invocation of democracy and the right to criticize one's government should be measured against the biased media coverage of local politics on a regular basis. The realization that the irregularities and corruption associated with some politicians are persistently ignored, whereas those associated with other politicians are continuously exposed, leads us to question the idea of democracy as the principle behind the góber precioso media frenzy. Instead, as D'Artígues suggests, we are in the presence of a phenomenon in which industry and culture merge in a frenzied strategy to increase ratings that uses the idea of democracy as a commodity.

The notion of democracy is open to the construction of its meaning; it is a screen upon which the most different economic and political ideas and aspirations can be projected. Thus, the global idea of democracy is continuously shaped and resignified as it is used in an attempt to validate a wide variety of local cultural practices. In the case of the góber precioso affair, democracy is tacitly made into an object of consumption, whereas cultural products associated with it, such as DJ Kermit's "Góber," are resignified as commodities no longer valid outside the larger media frenzy they come to articulate.

Musart's marketing of "Góber" shows this logic at work. The resignification of the track took place not only when the underground process of distribution was replaced by a mainstream marketing strategy but also in the very creation of versions aimed at a more profitable market than the one DJ Kermit originally tried to appeal to. The case of DJ Kermit's "Góber" is a glimpse into the glocal processes that give meaning to current DJ cultures and the complex ideological web that informs them. It is an intricate case that shows us that DJ cultures are often sites at which essentialist dichotomies collapse, global ideas are rewritten, and local culture offers the key to understand all of it.

Postlude: Back to the Góber Precioso Affair

In March 2006, soon after her kidnapping, Lydia Cacho sued the governor of Puebla in federal court for bribery, trafficking of influences, conspiracy to rape her, and abuse of authority. The result of that lawsuit as well as its legal consequences—news useless to the media once the political frenzy of 2006 was over—went largely unnoticed. On June 26, 2007, a special investigative commission from the Mexican Supreme Court determined that Marín and other authorities from Puebla had conspired against Lydia Cacho in order to benefit Kamel Nacif, but the passing of sentence by the ministers was delayed until November 29, 2007. At that time, and even though the court had ratified the resolution of the commission two days earlier, the final voting determined that "there is no proof that the human rights of journalist Lydia Cacho were violated" since the recording of telephone conversations has no legal value in a Mexican court.[25]

From February 14, 2006 (the day the infamous telephone conversation was made public), until the middle of 2007, the governor of Puebla spent more than USD $18 million to clear his public image. Most of this money made its way to a variety of media networks through the Social Communication area of the state of Puebla.[26] As propaganda showing Marín in a positive light inundated local and national media, and as Televisa and TV Azteca cancelled appearances by Cacho in their shows, the góber precioso affair slowly disappeared from newspaper headlines and television and radio airwaves.[27] Regardless of the effort of a few journalists—such as Carmen Aristegui, Carlos Loret de Mola, and Joaquín López Dóriga—the media that created a spectacle of "democracy" out of Marín and Nacif's conversation chose to ignore and render it invisible as money and political pressure touched the interests of the networks.

Ironically, the media's silencing of Cacho's voice took place just as the Supreme Court decided not to listen to the sounds of corruption that the entire country was hearing in determining the outcome of its investigation of the góber precioso affair. The silencing of sound seemed to be a strategy aimed at rendering the affair invisible in public space and making it disappear from the Mexican soundscape. However, sound is able to build and trigger memories and, just as memory as a collective background was necessary to allow for the irony in DJ Kermit's "Góber," the underground distribution of the track and the recordings are continuous reminders of the affair itself and the corruption practices surrounding it. Within the political and cultural context that nurtured the media spectacle of the góber precioso affair and its later invisibility, "Góber" is a sonic reminder of the contradictory relationship between media and state and of the emptiness and fragility of "democracy." As the silencing of the affair and Cacho's voice continue, it becomes a soundboard that loudly projects the disdain and fears Mexicans feel toward the elites who rule their country. In the end, the affair reminds us that under the cultural logic of untamed capitalism, which privileges the reproduction of the political and economic systems that guarantee the easiest and speediest reproduction of capital itself, more openness does not necessarily lead to more democracy. Instead, the relationship between media and politics becomes intricately interdependent, thus generating an array of cultural simulacra and media spectacles that inform one another and work as commodities while mediating and conditioning the relationship between individuals and these very representations (which individuals take as realities or unequivocal truths). Hence, entelechies such as "democracy" or "freedom of speech," powerful in the collective imagination but in fact empty of univocal meaning, are continuously reinvented in the production of spectacles.

The Sonics of Public Spaces

6

ALBA

Musical Temporality in the Carnival of Oruro, Bolivia

Gonzalo Araoz

THE CITY OF Oruro lies on the edge of an extensive steppe, at the foot of ten successive hills, in the northern part of the department of the same name, which is located in the highlands of western Bolivia. The city was founded on November 6, 1606, with the name Villa Real de San Felipe de Austria de Oruro.[1] The mineral richness of the hills and mountains drew the attention of Spanish conquerors searching for silver during the seventeenth century; by the late nineteenth century, the city of Oruro became, thanks to its strategic location, the most important mining and railroad center of the country.[2] However, the Great Depression and the Chaco War (1932–1935) marked the end of the expansion and capitalization of the mining industry, and most mines were finally closed by the mid-1980s.

Formerly known as an important mining, industrial, and railway center of the country, Oruro is today best known as the folklore capital of Bolivia, its Carnival parade being the most important social, cultural, and economic activity for which the population prepares throughout the year. UNESCO's declaration of the Oruro Carnival as an Intangible Cultural Heritage of Humanity produced a popular euphoria on May 18, 2001, when the local population watched the live transmission from Paris and the news was spontaneously celebrated by Orureños (people from Oruro) residing in different parts of the world.

According to Yves de la Menorval, who was UNESCO's representative in Bolivia at the time of this declaration, a particular feature of the intangible is that it is not necessarily linked to a physical heritage, and it can also be interpreted in different ways.[3] In relation to this, I have suggested, apart from its various interpretations, that the Oruro Carnival involves both the materialization of the intangible and the incorporation of physical-topographic features into the immaterial sphere of myth and dreams.[4] The incorporation of cultural and sociopolitical transformations into the spatial sphere of the festival has also been explored before.[5] In this chapter, I propose that the cultural intangibility of the festival could also clearly be identified in relation to its temporal and musical dimensions. Although the documents submitted by the Bolivian government to UNESCO do not specifically mention the musical temporality of the Oruro Carnival, they do underline the musical richness of the festival, an important component of Carnival temporality in the city of Oruro.

The Andean Carnival season extends from All Saints' Day in November until the end of Carnival in March. Although I will make reference to the importance of seasonal temporality for an understanding of the musical sphere of Carnival, my analysis will concentrate on the effects of music upon temporal perception through a description of the Alba rite (arguably the climax of the Oruro Carnival, during which hundreds of musicians play different Morenada tunes simultaneously), which takes place between the Saturday Carnival pilgrimage and the Sunday Carnival parade during late February or early March.[6] The celebration of Carnival is often interpreted as a dramatization of social-temporal processes in which the symbolic representation of time takes a central place. Such an approach contributes to the identification of different elements of analysis and to an understanding of complex phenomena in an orderly way. Although I recognize the value of such an approach, my own exploration of temporal perception in a specifically enhanced musical context demands the simultaneous discussion of specific features of the ritual process (such as the transformation of behavior according to the specific temporal phases of a ritual) and the practical organization and scheduling of such activities. I also incorporate ethnographic vignettes and personal memories within theoretical discussions to illustrate the ways in which different elements often overlap or merge together. Therefore, I start my exploration of musical-temporal perception by recalling a specific experience that has been particularly helpful in the processes of reflection on the contexts, issues, and perceptions involved in the temporal-musical sphere of Carnival.

About the Music in My Head

One afternoon in July 2000, as I was shopping in a street market in the city of Cochabamba, I heard someone shout, "*Oruro, Oruro!*" I turned around and saw a man marching on the pavement, both of his hands resting on his hips. He was lifting his knees, one at a time, and standing on the same spot, until he raised his right hand up and shouted again, "*Oruro, arrr arrr!*" He moved faster toward me. He jumped to the left, stopped again, continued to lift his knees, and then jumped to the right.

"Look at the Orureño," said the lady selling *moqochinchis* on the corner.[7] A man standing across the street whistled a Diablada tune, and other people laughed and started clapping to the rhythm. The dancer paused again, this time right in front of me. Although he was dressed in ordinary clothes, he used both hands to pull his (invisible) cape from above his shoulders. His eyes were fixed on the horizon, and he did not seem to be aware of the spectators' presence. "His head is full of Diablada," I thought and considered the possibility of joining his (imaginary) troupe of devil dancers, but other duties kept me from doing this. "Besides, my head is not full of Diablada but of Morenada."[8]

This image, apart from providing hints for the discussion of some issues related to the intangible sphere of Carnival, allows us to consider the occasional transcendence of a strictly demarcated spatial and temporal framework through the euphoric and popular celebration of the festival. The man seemed to be dancing at an inappropriate time and in an unusual place—it was not Carnival season and this did not happen in Oruro, the Bolivian capital of folklore. Although many of the dances displayed in the Oruro Carnival parade are also performed during festivals that take place at different times of the year and in different cities and towns, this particular performance was obviously enacted by a native from Oruro—who was either a visitor or a resident in the city of Cochabamba.[9] Even though the performance of Diablada is not restricted to Carnival season, the energetic performance of this devil dancer made clear reference to the famous

Carnival parade, which is deeply embedded in the minds of Orureños, wherever they may be.

The spatial and temporal "displacement" of the performance was coupled with an absence of the appropriate music. That is, this man was dancing the most traditional Carnival dance of Oruro in a different city, at a different time, without music, and without costume. Several months later, when I was writing my dissertation in the United Kingdom and transcribing the lyrics of the Morenada tune "Los Cocanis" into my ethnography, I found myself singing and dancing to this tune, which immediately installed itself back into my head. I felt the urge to dance, to drink, and to chew coca leaves, and this situation brought back the image of the dancer in Cochabamba. The long distance that separated me from the field during the time of "writing up" was in a way shortened by the "music in my head." Perhaps something similar happened to the man described above who, despite being away from his city and out of Carnival season, may have embodied the Carnival of Oruro without the need of a costume, mask, rattle, or brass band.

I will explain in the remainder of this chapter the phenomenon that I refer to as the "music in my head." At this point, it is sufficient to clarify that after years of attending the celebrations of Carnival in Oruro, the musical and choreographic rhythms of the festival seem to encroach upon the minds of the participants. After remembering the previously mentioned tune, for example, I needed to make an effort to ignore the music and concentrate on this sentence so I could type these words. As suggested, rhythm and memory are relevant to the exploration of temporal perception,[10] which I will discuss mainly in relation to the performance of Morenada tunes during the enactment of the Alba rite in the Carnival of Oruro. Let us first review some concepts that are often considered to be linked to the notion of time.

The Puzzle of Time

According to Richard Gale, the problem of time refers to a corpus of intimately related questions concerning truth, knowledge, events, causality, identification, action, and change.[11] Using these concepts—and many others, such as motion, repetition, and succession—scholars have struggled to define time through millennia. Although time constitutes a completely familiar dimension of our daily lives, any attempt to define it introduces endless puzzles that might be related to its overall relation to life and death, as much as to its intangibility. I will discuss these issues in relation to the temporal and musical dimensions of Carnival in the city of Oruro, but it is necessary to begin with a brief consideration of the symbolic representation of time, given its central place in anthropological studies of Carnival.

Edmund Leach asserts that repetition and irreversibility constitute two notions that are inherent to our modern understanding of time. According to Leach, repetition marks each interval of time, which also has a beginning and an end. He argues that religious dogmas have the tendency to deny the irreversibility of time by replacing it with the (opposite) concept of repetition. That is, for example, equating death with birth.[12] In his second essay on the symbolic representation of time, Leach asserts that among those societies where there are no calendars of the nautical almanac type, the progress of a year is marked by a succession of festivals. Each festival represents a temporary transit from the normal/profane sphere to the abnormal/sacred sphere of experience and back again.[13] This gives rise to four distinct phases or states of the "moral person" (sacralization, marginal state, desacralization, and normal secular life) and three distinct kinds of ritual behavior (formality, masquerade, and role reversal).[14]

Leach considers formality and masquerade as a pair of contrasted oppositions, whereas role reversal is seen as symbolizing a complete transference from the secular to the sacred.[15] Role reversal is thus explained in reference to the logical opposition between the state of normal secular life and the marginal state, symbolically represented in the performative reversed behavior of social actors.

Max Gluckman argues that, although such rites of reversal may include a protest against the established order, they are intended to preserve and even strengthen it.[16] On the other hand, Victor Turner considers the liminal period (or marginal state) as constituting a phase of antistructure and long periods of liminality, which lead to the creation of social togetherness—*communitas*.[17] The symbolic-performative sphere of Carnival and other ritually enhanced festivities is thus linked to the actual creation of a sense of community. Turner suggests that the "orchestrations of media" that are often found in major ritual performances do not refer to the emission of a single message through different media but rather to subtly variant messages, which result in "a hall of magic mirrors, each interpreting as well as reflecting the images beamed to it."[18] Therefore, apart from a possible multivocality, we must also consider different sensory codes and probably also synesthesia. This may be experienced in Oruro, where the participant can perceive the fusion of images, textures, sounds, smells, and tastes. We will concentrate on the effects of music upon temporal perception during the celebration of the Alba rite, but first let us briefly review the philosophical and anthropological literature on temporal perception and discuss it in relation to the musical sphere of the Carnival celebrations in Oruro.

Temporal Perception

D. H. Mellor asserts that our perception of the flow of time is only an accumulation of memories and that the flow of time takes us into the future (rather than the past) because a memory is an effect (not a cause) of what is remembered. According to him, causal order fixes temporal order, distinguishing it from spatial order. This is to say that causes precede their effects in time rather than in space.[19] Alfred Gell draws on Mellor's philosophy of time to reject metaphysical assumptions based on ethnographic research, underlining that mundane social processes constitute the background for the ritual reconstruction of the world according to human desires. Though it is accepted that rituals dramatize and even manipulate time, they do not create or modify it, except rhetorically or symbolically.[20] Gell also emphasizes the importance of distinguishing time from the events that happen in time, as well as the interplay between objective and subjective aspects of temporality, which requires the development of a theory of time cognition.

Husserl's theory is, according to Gell, the most careful and intricate account of subjective time available to us. Both Brentano (Husserl's teacher) and Husserl use musical examples to explain the problem of continuity of the subjective/perceptual present and the model of internal time consciousness, respectively.[21] Husserl illustrates the complexity of temporal perception by examining some of the processes through which we listen to a melody: "While the first tone is sounding, the second comes, then the third, and so on. Must we not say that when the second tone sounds I hear *it*, but I no longer hear the first, and so on? In truth, therefore, I do not hear the melody but only the particular tone which is actually present. . . . [Furthermore,] every tone itself has a temporal extension: With its continued sounding, however, it has an ever new now, and the tone actually preceding is changing into something past. Therefore, I hear at any instant only the actual phase of the tone."[22] Brentano had already partially explained the perception of a temporally continuous time-object in relation to the (also musically related) following question: How can we hear a continuous tone played in an oboe for five seconds as a continuous duration? He supposed, "That we only hear the now-present tone, but that we enrich this hearing with 'associations' derived from earlier hearing-experiences in the sequence."[23]

In relation to such associations, Husserl introduces the concepts of *retention* and *protention,* distinguishing the former from *reproduction,* which is an action-replay of past experiences of events. Although retentions are what we have of temporally removed parts of experiences (from the "now" moment), protentions are their future-oriented counterparts.[24] Therefore, retentions and protentions form the horizon of a temporally extended present, where the "knife edge now" is replaced by the "thick present."[25] Retentions and protentions should not be thought of as fixed and static but as dynamic. Thus, as the present progresses, the past changes its significance, and it is evaluated differently, according to the development of present events. Gell suggests that perspectival diminutions and attenuations could be a powerful metaphor to explain this process but that we should be aware of the differences between temporal perspective and visual perspective. The former is related mainly to the sphere of time and memory, whereas the latter refers mainly to the sphere of space and vision.[26]

In a posterior work, Gell evaluates how his own visually oriented notion of reality prevented him (during fieldwork in Melanesia) from understanding the Umedas' distinctive perceptual framework, because they defined objective existence in terms of audibility.[27] A similar reflection should prevent us from imposing the visual bias that is characteristic of the anthropological gaze so we can allow ourselves to perceive and describe the temporal/audible sphere of events, which is specifically useful for an exploration of the musical temporality in the Carnival of Oruro.

The cacophonic context of the Alba rite demands an approach that considers both musical and temporal dimensions, and this highlights the relevance of Victor Zuckerkandl's work. The philosopher of music Zuckerkandl conceives music as a temporal art[28] in the sense that in it, time reveals itself to experience. According to Zuckerkandl, the feeling of rhythm— taken as a genuine experience—is the experience (or even the cognition) of time itself. This approach can be extremely relevant to understanding temporal perception during the Alba rite in Oruro, when the notions of succession, pause, repetition, time, rhythm, and memory are often musically blurred together.

Musical Temporality

Hans Meyerhoff points out the need to contextualize the questions we ask about time, and he highlights the irreconcilability between time in experience and time in nature, which leads to divergent philosophical interpretations. Experienced (subjective) time differs radically from the regular, uniform, and quantitative units of an objective metric.[29] Meyerhoff considers that the human mind can be thought of as a recording instrument and that memory relations, unlike time in nature, exhibit a non-uniform, dynamic order of events: "Things remembered are fused and confused with things feared and hoped for. Wishes and fantasies may not only be remembered as facts, but the facts remembered are constantly modified, reinterpreted and re-lived in the light of the present exigencies, past fears, and future hopes."[30]

Victor Zuckerkandl also underlines the differences between the musical and the physical concepts of time. Although the physical concept takes time as order and form of experience, the musical concept takes it as content of experience. Physical time measures events and is—according to physics and its models—divisible into equal parts, but musical time produces events and knows no equality of parts. The musical existence of time is the same as its activity; meter and rhythm are the effects of the flow of time in the tones: "Because tones have duration, because time elapses in them, and for no other reason, we have the rhythm of our music. Only time can be the agent and source of the forces active in meter and rhythm."[31] Such a musical concept of time makes it possible to compare Husserl's "protentions" with a "musical-temporal anticipation": "Our foreknowledge is concerned with the stream of events; our hearing is concerned with the stream of time. So far as I know and represent to myself what is to come, I do not hear; and so far as I hear, I do not know and do not represent to myself what is to come."[32]

This does not necessarily run against Husserl's arguments, for he also specified that protentions are not representations of the future but rather some sort of temporal (and musical) anticipation. Husserl's theory of internal time consciousness, along with many of the concepts generally linked to the definitions of time, become more comprehensible in relation to musical rhythm in the light of Zuckerkandl's work. Motion, then, cannot be without time: "Motion in a realm from which things and space are absent is, thanks to music, a substantiated fact; motion in a realm from which time is absent is self-contradictory."[33]

The succession of beats and the duration of tones are also explained in reference to the flow of time, taking into account the combination of progression and recurrence in the notion of temporal succession. Finally, Zuckerkandl states that musicians (as opposed to philosophers and psychologists) are led, from their observations, to opposite conclusions: "*Change* does not create time; time literally creates *change*."[34] The discussion of such a philosophical dilemma lies beyond the scope of this chapter. However, the concepts of motion, succession, progression, recurrence, and change will underpin my exploration of (altered) temporal perception through musical performance in the Carnival of Oruro.

Musical-Temporal Perception in Oruro

The celebration of Carnival marks, within a broader yearly festive cycle, the end of the rainy season in the Andes. According to Olivia Harris, the Laymi,[35] for example, divide the year "into two contrasted halves, each marked by a feast of the dead; one half is a time for sorrow and hard work, while the other is dedicated to feasting, pleasure and rest from their labours."[36] Despite the notable differences between the ways in which All Saints' Day and Carnival are celebrated in rural and urban Bolivian contexts, there are also some common features of these feasts that, according to Harris, are perceived by the Laymi as *muntu intiru,* or worldwide celebrations. All Saints' Day is a spring festival that marks the time for sowing and planting and the start of the rains in the Andes, and Carnival marks the end of the rains and the harvest of the new year's first fruits.[37]

The distinctive features of such calendrical rites are enhanced by the musical sphere of the feasts. Harris points out that All Saints' Day initiates the time of *wayñus*—"melodies played on wooden flutes (*tarkas*) whose explicitly mournful tones pervade the whole season and attract rain"[38]— and stresses that it is through music that she realized how the souls of the dead are believed to remain in the world of the living throughout the rainy season. Thus, the flutes that provide the mournful melodies during the rainy season are piled together after performing a ritual dispatch of the dead (represented by devil dancers among the Laymi), and *charangos* (small mandolin-like instruments made of armadillo shells) are then used to perform a radically different musical style (*kirki*). This marks not only the end of the rainy season but also the departure of the dead, which proscribes the performance of wayñus and the use of tarkas at this dramatic point of time. Harris explains that this is due to the fact that "flute music attracts rain;[39] it is a form of dirge and thus will not cause offence to the dead, whose co-operation is essential to bring the crops to fruition. In stark contrast, the music of the dry season is joyful and celebratory. The wayñu music of the rainy season is said to weep (*q'asi*) while the kirki of the dry season is happy (*kusisi*)."[40] Similarly, Henry Stobart suggests that music, as the culturally determined formation of sound, constitutes an appropriate basis for the analysis of cultural and cognitive categories and concepts of growth and regeneration in the Andes. Thus, sound may be equated with the animation of living beings, since musical performance is an essential and generative part of life.[41] Stobart shows how distinctive musical instruments, tunings, and genres are understood to directly influence climatic conditions and plant growth.

Some propitiatory rites are also performed in urban areas through mimetic acts that, although in some cases are closer to the rural traditions, generally hold little (if any) resemblance to the latter. The participation of musicians playing traditional Andean musical instruments does not constitute a main feature of the Carnival parade. The overwhelming majority of brass instruments during Carnival 2000, for example, clearly illustrates the predominance of brass bands and the comparatively small proportion of tarkas and other traditional instruments. That year, 105 brass bands (with a total number of 4,010 musicians) participated in the Entrada, whereas only five groups played traditional Andean musical instruments (which could not have surpassed 200 musicians).[42]

However, many of the musicians who play brass instruments in Oruro also play traditional instruments in their rural villages. Indeed, some of the most popular modern rhythms of the Oruro Carnival are said to have their origins in traditional music performed in rural contexts. For example, Don Juan Zapana,[43] a prolific composer of Morenada tunes, asserts that the Morenada developed as a slight modification of wayñu but that it actually has a rhythm of its own. He argues that composing Morenadas is not as easy as it seems, because the rhythm has to be accurately paired and balanced.

Don Juan was born in 1953 in the community Villa Kairiri of the Umala cantonment in the Department of La Paz. Both of his parents were also from Umala, and they migrated to Oruro in the 1930s. All their relatives moved to Oruro during the 1920s, in order to commercialize coca leaf, alcohol, and aniline dyeing powder. They organized themselves and created a musical group, playing the tarkas. Don Juan learned to play the instrument in Kairiri when he was young, and he later heard about the Morenada from the Cocanis (coca leaf traders), his relatives with whom he also learned to play and compose Morenadas with brass instruments.

According to the historian Juan Carlos Estenssoro, trumpets were introduced early during Spanish colonial times in the Andes, a region where music was considered an important element of political representation.[44] The Spanish trumpets that first caused awe among the local population were later used by indigenous authorities as a sign of power and prestige— transmitted in a hereditary way and used, together with other Western instruments, to demonstrate the power of the Caciques (local indigenous authorities). Estenssoro asserts that the Catholic Church, since its arrival during the sixteenth century, was in charge of controlling musical performances. Initially, this entailed the introduction of Western instruments, as well as the prohibition to perform music that was considered profane.[45] However, given the apparent impossibility of eliminating the fiestas, colonial authorities searched for ways to regulate them, keep them under control, and ensure that such cultural manifestations were directed to the "true God."[46] Thus, through the incorporation of Andean fiestas into the colonial system, the Church managed to absorb them as another institution of the new regime, transforming an important part of its forms and contents.[47]

During the twentieth century, indigenous musical instruments and themes had been used in a process of "folklorization" characteristic of a nationalist ideology. Brass instruments were also appropriated by groups of urban indigenous migrants. Buechler explains how the introduction of brass bands into the fiestas celebrated in the community of Compi, on the shores of Lake Titicaca, was the outcome of expanding social networks and increased intra- and interregional contact between peasants and mestizos:[48] "The history of brass bands... indicates a step-by-step acceleration in the formation of intraregional ties, and is both the product and a metaphor of expanding networks. It has its musical manifestation in the remarkable homogeneity of modern Aymara and Quechua music, a sameness which is counter-balanced only by the fact that brass bands everywhere are expanding their repertoires and the more innovative bands are introducing new tunes."[49]

As previously mentioned, the musical sphere of Carnival season in the city of Oruro is marked by an absolute predominance of brass bands. One probable exception could refer to the private parties held in different houses and clubs around the city, where brass bands may be replaced by other musical groups that use electronic instruments.[50] Late in the evening on Carnival Saturday (during the early hours of Carnival Sunday), when all dance groups hold such private parties, a distinct, more popular, and public affair takes place. It is the Alba rite that, I would argue, encapsulates the popular celebration and musical frenzy of the Oruro Carnival.

Alba

The tumultuous Alba rite takes place between Saturday evening and Sunday morning during the weekend of Carnival. However, I must stress that this entails more than just a fixed position of the event within the schedule of local celebrations. I would argue that it is not possible to determine exactly when the Alba rite starts and ends. In 2000, for example, it started before the Saturday pilgrimage was over, and in 2002, it had not yet finished when the Sunday parade approached the Plaza del Folklore, at the foot of the temple where the performances end. Given its "intermediate position" between the official Catholic pilgrimage of Saturday and the more popular (and pagan) Sunday parade, this rite could be interpreted as a threshold or as representing the phase of desacralization, in Leach's terms.[51]

The temporality of the Alba rite can be addressed at different levels. I shall first consider a macroscopic view of its temporal location within the general Carnival celebrations. The "intermediate position" (between Saturday and Sunday) of this tumultuous event denotes its temporal liminality within the official schedule; it does not belong to Saturday or Sunday. At the same time, this enables the Alba rite to transform—through its performance—the event that precedes it and the one that follows it.

Both the Saturday pilgrimage and the Sunday parade always require some kind of order and form. They also tend to be divisible, much like the aforementioned physical concept of time.[52] The Alba rite, like the musical concept of time, does not depend on any strict order and form. It is not divisible, and, I would argue, it constitutes the content of experience. As Zuckerkandl suggests, the musical existence of time is the same as its activity—meter and rhythm are the effects of the flow of time in the musical tones.[53] Although some may object that there is an important meaning in the Alba rite,[54] I would stress that its strength resides in its actual performance.

Early on Carnival Sunday, the Plaza del Folklore, at the foot of the Temple of the Virgin of the Mineshaft—where the Alba rite takes place—is crammed with people dancing, singing, eating, and drinking in a tumultuous and chaotic gathering. Perhaps it is easier to visualize the effectiveness of this event in spatial terms,[55] but the works of Husserl and Zuckerkandl on temporal cognition and musical temporality, respectively, contribute adequate conceptual tools for an approach to its temporal dimension.[56] As I have suggested, the Alba rite transforms—through its chaotic enactment—the orderly events that precede and follow it. The last dance groups and the first dance groups participating in the Saturday and Sunday parades, respectively, encounter upon their arrival at the Plaza del Folklore the chaotic and drunken crowd that forces them to alter their performances at the final stage. The site, which is strictly reserved for the dancers earlier on Saturday and later on Sunday, has been temporarily appropriated by the inebriated revelers. The temporal liminality of the Alba rite encroaches upon the official schedule of Carnival, denoting a "specious present," or a "thick present" in Husserl's terms. This achieves even greater complexity when one considers the musical framework, which is constructed through the multitudinous performance of the Morenada rhythm.

There are different interpretations of the Morenada, but all of them underline the representation of African slaves through dance. This is expressed in the dance steps as much as in the masks, costumes, and rattles that are used by the dancers. The great weight of the Moreno costume forces dancers to move slowly and balance their bodies with short steps of two and three movements to either side.[57] "Movements forward and backwards, complete and three-quarter turns, and positions of the feet that contribute to the general cadence of the group that collectively displays a sinister progression towards death."[58] The dancers use a rattle (or other noisemaker) to mark the rhythm and signal a change in the choreography. It is believed that the short steps of the dancers represent the difficult movements of the African slaves who had to drag along the weight of the chains around their feet. The classic clattering sound of the rattles is a reminiscence of the crucial long walks forced upon the "black pieces" in their introduction from Panama to the Andes,[59] with the continuous creaking of the old carriages and heavy chains. The Moreno masks clearly resemble African slaves, but they have exaggerated features such as bulging eyes and enormous lips and tongues.

African slaves were imported to the Andes during the sixteenth century, and it has been suggested that most of them were captured in Angola and collectively blessed in Luanda by Catholic priests in preparation for their long and tragic journey.[60] Since the Africans could not adapt to the high altitude of the mines in Potosí and Oruro, they were transported to the valleys and foothills of the Andes—mainly for the production of coca leaf.[61]

Every year during the Alba rite, between twelve and fifteen brass bands play different Morenada tunes simultaneously. This slow and cadenced rhythm (2/4) can be compared to the oscillation of a pendulum, clearly marking its own temporality. This is enhanced through the use of noise-makers; the dancers often turn the handles—which are connected to the gear teeth inside the rattle—in short movements that resemble both the tick-tock and the winding of a clock. Spectators tend to dance, clap, and shout along to the rhythm marked by the rattles. The repetitive musical and choreographic performances of Morenada rhythm can be interpreted as the flow of Carnival time in Oruro.

There are two "gaps" within Morenada rhythm. One refers to a slight "stretching" of a tone that demands a short halt, a sudden double beat, or a slight and brief alteration of the tempo to immediately start over again. The other refers to a silence after a stanza and before a chorus. This silence is filled with a playful comment by the trombones (playing either a single prolonged and distorted tone or the same tone in repetitive fashion) or the voices of performers and spectators (a vocalized version of the trombone notes), before the main rhythm and melody returns. Although these gaps may seem to distort the "clockwork rhythm" of Morenada, they tend to signal a new start. The concepts of motion, succession, progression, recurrence, and change are all present in this rhythm. However, the simultaneous interpretation of different Morenada tunes during the Alba rite contributes to the musical construction of a chaotic scenario and temporality through cacophony. Anthony Seeger suggests that music is also defined by what it is not: silence.[62] Apart from measuring rhythm, silence also creates rhythm. If silence and rhythm are fundamental musical-temporal features (one creates and is created by the other), how must we consider their absence (or excess, in the case of rhythm) during the Alba rite?

Tens of thousands of people participate in the Alba rite every year, and most (if not all) of them dance Morenada and use rattles. However, though the marked temporality of each Morenada tune may still be perceived within the immediate surroundings of the performing band, the general cacophony produced by the musicians does not allow for the distinction of motion, succession, progression, recurrence, and change. Their fusion creates a peculiar temporality in which the "specious" or "thick" present described by Husserl is prolonged for many hours, without a specific protention or retention. Every instant of silence within a particular Morenada tune is saturated by the loudness produced by other bands playing in the vicinity. There is neither a specific musical anticipation of what is to come nor is there a musical memory of what just passed, because there is an excessive input of rhythmic information.

The predictable rhythm of Morenada becomes unpredictable during this event, as each pause in the rhythm (which would normally mark a new start and, therefore, motion, succession, progression, recurrence, and change) is saturated with the noise of hundreds of trumpets, tubas, trombones, drums, cymbals, and a roaring and generally inebriated crowd. However, despite my inability to distinguish such temporal features in a short-term musical memory during the Alba rite, the excessive input of sound had a dramatic effect on my long-term musical memory. Several times, I found myself looking around for the (nonexistent) bands performing the Morenadas in my mind, up to ten days after the event. I was frightened the first time this happened because I could not explain where the music (that only I heard) came from. Later, I got used to this, to the extent that once, I was surprised when someone commented about music performed by a band in the vicinity—I thought that it was only playing in my mind!

I never found another person who had similar experiences as many days after the festival, but some agreed that they heard Morenadas in their heads while celebrating Carnival in Oruro. I must clarify an important detail at this point: it appears that I unwittingly submitted myself to an experiment by using headphones to listen closely to the music that I recorded in the Oruro Carnival, particularly during the Alba rite. It is possible that the amplified loudness through the use of headphones enhanced the (similar but milder) effects that other participants told me they perceived during

Carnival in Oruro. Needless to say, such euphoric and tumultuous celebrations also entail a sense of closeness and community on one hand and violent confrontations on the other, which I have explored elsewhere.[63] Time, space, and place seemed to chaotically merge every time I participated in the Alba rite, and I would argue that the extraordinary sonorous sphere of the Alba rite, far from providing a backdrop for the celebration of this particular event, constitutes the sound of the intangible and transcendent temporality of the celebration of Carnival in the city of Oruro.

7

Such a Noise!

Fireworks and the Soundscapes
of Two Veracruz Festivals

Andrew Grant Wood

They cheered when the rockets went up, they danced with each other in the
crowd, and then had gone off a little way by themselves and danced again,
the jota, the malagueña, the bolero, playing their castanets.
—Katherine Anne Porter, *Ship of Fools*

AFTER MOVING FROM Montreal to Kalamazoo, Michigan, my family and I
heartily embraced the use of firecrackers in the late 1960s and early 1970s as
we anticipated the U.S. national Fourth of July holiday. The process began
each year during Easter vacation jaunts to Florida, with short stopovers at
roadside stands in Georgia that sold a wide variety of pyrotechnics. Planning for the summer celebration, we eagerly stocked up on Black Cat brand
firecrackers, bottle rockets, Roman candles, flying saucers, and smoke
bombs. When the July holiday finally arrived, youthful afternoons were
spent circulating through the neighborhood, gleefully detonating noisy
firecrackers and shooting off screaming bottle rocket sorties while also
conspiring to set clouds of stinky green, yellow, and red smoke in the air.
The arrival of adult cocktail hour then meant it was time for an impromptu
firecracker war between the Wood family and our next-door neighbors the
Trubees.

At the appointed time, the go-ahead for a ritualistic volley was given.
The Trubees armed themselves exclusively with their favored cherry

bombs, and the Woods did likewise with an assortment of small explosives. A battle raged for ten minutes or so across our shared lots—a flurry of small, fiery explosives sounded a cacophonic chorus and unleashed a rain of wrapping paper into the air and clouds of smelly sulfur smoke into the row of bushes between our adjoining side yards. When two groups had consumed the requisite amount of ammunition, a truce was called as a few last firecrackers popped and sputtered. Upon reflection, I guess we were lucky no one got hurt or was slapped by the local police with a stiff fine.[1] As it turns out, our noisy neighborly get-together not only resonated with other U.S. national celebrations taking place elsewhere but also drew upon an international tradition of public celebrations that stretched back hundreds, if not thousands, of years.

Fireworks are virtually synonymous with civic and religious festival making. Their spectacular, colorful sights; sizzling rocket sounds; and bombastic explosions—not to mention pungent smell—provide extraordinary sensory (and mnemonic) stimulation for millions of people around the world each year. Fireworks are also widely deployed in the service of religious observations around the world. New Year's Eve, Carnival, and various saints' days are all occasions during which pyrotechnic displays are deployed to add significance and mark holiday, even sacred, time. Although reception varies greatly, pyrotechnic practices clearly play an important role in fomenting shared social meaning and inclusive community identity. Carefully considered, the various social and cultural contexts in which they are deployed also hold potential as a historical source material.[2]

In this chapter, I consider the significance of fireworks in two popular public celebrations in the state of Veracruz, Mexico. The first is Carnival in the modern, industrial port of Veracruz. Pyrotechnics used during Carnival help anticipate the upcoming forty days of fasting during Lent by helping to create a momentary period of temporary social disorder and ribald celebration. Somewhat in contrast, Candelaria is a festival cast as a more traditional and explicitly religious gathering. For this, organizers use fireworks to denote festival time and space. In doing so, they mark symbolically larger processes for participants that encompass a cycle of birth, death, and renewal. With their vibrant sonic, visual, and olfactory character, fireworks in both events help foster a public sense of celebration and rejuvenation through an imagined purification rite as negative "spirits" are banished.[3]

Chinese Cooking, Flag Waving, and Noise

The invention and initial development of fireworks as a communications medium and subsequent commercial industry took shape in the Chinese province of Hunan. As legend has it, the first fireworks came when a Chinese chef accidentally dropped saltpeter in a nearby cooking fire (therefore adding the requisite charcoal and sulfur) some two thousand years ago. Nearly a millennium later, a Chinese monk named Li Tian (also in Hunan Province) engaged in a more intentional fashioning of firecrackers: gunpowder in bamboo shoots.[4]

Fireworks soon took center stage in a variety of social gatherings. Weddings, funerals, religious holidays, and business openings are all suitable occasions for their use. They were also incorporated by the Chinese into home life as it became traditional to string them (and even set them off) indoors in order to bring about "new beginnings, harmony, balance, fame, wealth, awareness, energizing of the lazy, comfort for all, and protection of the household from harm."[5]

Before long, European visitors to Asia got in on the act. As pyrotechny came to the West, the practice first became popular in Italy sometime during the fifteenth century and then spread to Spain, France, Russia, Denmark, and England. Historian Alan St. H. Brock details a variety of European celebrations such as royal births, marriages, and coronations where fireworks were employed.[6]

Shortly after the reign of Elizabeth I in England, for example, the celebration of Guy Fawkes Day on November 5 (which commemorates the thwarting of a pro-Catholic conspiracy to bomb Parliament in 1605) would prove especially ripe for fireworks. Subsequent celebrations eventually toned down the antipapist furor in favor of evening pranks and the burning of Fawkes effigies stuffed with firecrackers.[7] Following this, journalists, writers, painters, and others recorded the growing popularity of fireworks displays and development.[8]

During the Fourth of July festivities in the United States, fireworks have long been meant to evoke feelings of patriotism and national identity. They are thought to dramatize as *feu d'artifice* the military struggle that took place between the British and Americans during the American Revolution. In the early nineteenth century, as the young republic went to war once again with England, Francis Scott Key's "The Star Spangled Banner" further added patriotic imagery to the growing tradition, as the lyrics ("And the rocket's red glare, the bombs bursting in air / Gave proof through the night that our flag was still there") portray a critical struggle in early national history.[9] Describing the military encounter with rockets glaring red and bombs bursting, the ode to the national flag is a testament to U.S. heroism made all the more poignant through the allusion to specific battle sights and sounds. Today, great effort and expense goes into producing these pyrotechnic performances not just in the United States but also elsewhere around the world.[10] Official and unofficial fireworks displays often assume a central role in a variety of national celebrations. As such, they are meant to commemorate historical events, statehood, and civic authority.

Though officially understood to reference serious issues of social and political history, pyrotechnics are also intended to be pleasurable—even mischievously fun—because of their ability to disrupt our senses and, on certain occasions, legitimately create a temporary public disturbance. Their visceral shock and awe provide a kind of perceptual intervention that in a festival environment may encourage social bonding and community identification. The noise, flash, and smell of fireworks are understandably deployed for celebratory purposes and the sheer onslaught they render upon one's senses issues a stimulation and subsequent release from that which temporarily alters our perception of time and motion. Discussing the influence of noise in this regard, one scholar writes: "Noise brings you to your body, your body without organs, perhaps, but also a body made ear. When noise occurs, listening gives way to hearing, giving way in turn to the loss of hearing—not literally, but in the sense of losing the ability to distinguish sounds, to keep sounds as a merely auditory input. The volume and harshness of the sounds bring your body to be, in noise, even in the loss of awareness."[11] The pyrotechnic display is not unlike what one experiences during a musical performance. If the show is produced to be outsized and noisy, confrontational, and perhaps even intended to overwhelm the senses, then a possible transformative outcome is being programmed—one in which the spectator imagines that he or she is engaged in an extraordinary experience. Rather than solely a contemporary occurrence, however, this is a situation in which people have long participated.

Looking and Listening for Fireworks in Mexican History

Mexican cultural theorist Néstor García Canclini writes that fiestas (and, by extension, other public celebrations) generally exist to preserve social order through inclusion. "The fiesta is not an outrageous liberation of instincts, as so many phenomenologists and anthropologists have thought, but a demarcated place and time in which the rich must pay for everybody's pleasure and in which everybody's pleasure is moderated by 'social interest.' [Even] the parodies of power, the irreverent questioning of order (during Carnival) are tolerated in spaces and times and exceptionality lead back to routine."[12] Civic and religious rituals, despite occasional appearances to the contrary, generally serve to reinforce social hierarchy and power. On this, anthropologist Stanley Brandes observes that the use of fireworks in Mexican society can be understood as a "celebration of power" as towns and cities that take part in community displays articulate their social status while also encouraging civic identification.[13]

Mexicans have long deployed pyrotechnics to mark important civic and religious occasions. Fireworks were used, for example, to articulate expressions of loyalty to the king or for marking a change in government.[14] Pyrotechnic displays are also a part of other celebrations, including local saints' days, funeral processions, Three Kings' Day, Carnival, Holy Week (with accompanying Judas burnings), and Independence Day.[15]

Traditionally, construction of fireworks in Mexico reveals two basic types.[16] There are the more visually oriented castles (*castillos*) and waterfalls of light (*lluvias de luce* or *cascadas*), as well as the noisemaking skyrockets (*cohetes*).[17] Stressing the important role that the cohetes play with their resounding acoustic power, Brandes suggests that, on occasion, they also serve as a religious medium. Here, he relates that one of his informants believed "cohetes carry our message, our prayers, rapidly up to heaven."[18] Still another source commented about the fact that when he heard the sound of the skyrockets, he knew that an "important religious ritual had begun and that he felt compelled to participate."[19] Taken along with the alluring light display pyrotechnics, powerful noise producing fireworks resoundingly make their presence felt in much festival production.

My quest to document the use and significance of pyrotechnics in Mexico began in December 2003 when I learned of an unfortunate fireworks-related fire in the port of Veracruz. Apparently, the municipal government had granted permission for the sale of firecrackers during the year-end holiday time, and on December 29, a man got careless with a lit cigarette and accidentally set a fireworks vending stand across from the municipal market on fire. Hundreds of firecrackers suddenly exploded, and soon several parked cars got swept up in the conflagration. Before firefighters managed to bring the situation under control, a nearby shoe store, paint store, fabric store, and several other businesses went up in flames. Ultimately, the fire destroyed a significant amount of property and caused much alarm.[20] An ensuing proclamation by the Veracruz city government officially banned the sale and informal use of fireworks altogether. Intrigued by this incident, I set out to try and document the resonance of fireworks in Veracruz history.

In colonial Mexico, vice regal decrees banning the production of fireworks, along with the unofficial transport of gunpowder within the city walls, can be traced back to 1610. With the city largely constructed out of wood (*ciudad de tablas*), the threat of fire represented a significant danger. Subsequent allusions to fireworks (*fuegos artificiales*) throughout the remainder of the colonial period generally consist of a few permissions granted to entrepreneurs for specific usage during holiday time.[21]

Apart from the occasional mention in local archival records, several travelers who made their way around the state of Veracruz also commented on the use of pyrotechnics. Visiting Mexico in the late 1880s, Jesuit Charles Croonenbergs made his way to the industrial city of Orizaba in late September and early October. He briefly describes a celebration dedicated to the Virgin at which hundreds of people, including many from indigenous groups, gathered outside a local church. Croonenbergs delights in the lively sights and sounds including "firecracker displays launched from the roofs of nearby buildings."[22]

In 1925, Danish traveler Franz Blom and American Oliver la Farge went to Mexico. Making their way to the southern Los Tuxtlas area of the state, they visited the indigenous village of Tatahuicapa. Arriving on the eve of a celebration honoring the local patron saint, the travelers noted the festive dress, architectural adornments, and noisemaking of the locals who "are always lighting off firecrackers." Their first night in town, loud explosions meant to mark the opening of Tatahuicapa's festival awoke the two around two o'clock in the morning.[23] Apparently not unusual at the time, Blom and la Farge also comment on the regular use of firecrackers by indigenous residents in the neighboring town of San Martín Pajapan.[24] In these and no doubt many other popular religious celebratory circumstances, villagers deployed arrhythmic, explosive pyrotechnic sound.

Louisiana poet and novelist Mary Ashley Townsend spent time in Orizaba during the late nineteenth century and had the opportunity to observe an Independence Day celebration. In a wonderfully descriptive passage worth quoting at length, she writes

> At about nine o'clock a large concourse filled the main street, and every man, woman and boy carried a banner of green, white and red, on a long bamboo. Presently men with torches began to appear and at last everyone had a torch in one hand and a little flag in the other. Then mammoth transparencies appeared, magnified representations of such as one sees anywhere on similar occasions, then Roman candles began to turn and powder lights to burn.... Rockets were now set up, and there were loud calls for the Governor. He seemed to enjoy the unlimited popularity [as] he appeared upon his balcony and made a speech which was received with signs of great approval. He was frequently interrupted by shouts of applause and salvos of fireworks which seemed to go off in a frenzy of approbation. In every instance as their crackling and rattling died out the echoing mountains caught up the sound repeating it near and far.... Then came a gang of workmen who planted immense batteries of fireworks at certain distances apart along the middle of the street. There were towers and triangles and wheels and serpents and arches and above them all rose stupendous affairs which people called "castles in the air." These were a combination of all the other devices and were quite new to my rather limited experience in pyrotechnic architecture. When one after another of these were set off it was not difficult to believe the world had exploded. Such a noise! Such whizzing, and fizzing, and shooting, and floods of fire and avalanches of sparks and everything apparently going in an opposite direction to everything else all at the same time! In the meanwhile were sent off rockets and bombs and "bouquets" and Roman candles which roofed the town with flashes of flame their green, white and red lights braiding themselves together in the zenith to untangle, as they fell, into strands of glowing fire which melted into darkness only to be renewed again and again. It was past midnight when we closed our massive doors against the boom of the last bomb, the hiss of the last rocket, the last burst of strange music.[25]

Townsend's colorful account makes clear not only the dazzling displays of light but also the central role pyrotechnic "noise" played in community celebration. Her writing is propelled by sound as she writes "Such a noise! Such whizzing, and fizzing, and shooting" to describe the raucous scene.[26]

Another Independence Day observance was considered by French anthropologist Jacques Soustelle. Soustelle spent time in Veracruz in September 1932. There, on one particular night, Soustelle describes the plaza filled with people, music, and light. At the appointed hour, he writes how the mayor sounded the independence call (*grito*), which then signaled the start of "a thousand explosions, the lighting of *castillos*, along with the launching of hundreds of large firecrackers and skyrockets." Recalling Mary Ashley Townsend's earlier amazement, "the castillos," Soustelle writes, "are two meters high and send a magnificent wave of light and ash over the crowd." This was followed by the launching of red and green rockets whose sizzle, smoke, and appearance were much appreciated by those assembled who *ooh*, *ahh*, laugh, and clap enthusiastically. Soustelle continues: "Firecrackers explode over the cafes in the Portales with flashes reflecting off the buildings and faces of the parishioners." Finally, the visiting Frenchman observes that "during the display, everyone [was] in a good mood, smiling like devils while the plaza is bathed in light."[27] Again, sound and smell, although not so explicitly remarked upon, nevertheless add significantly to the visual effect.

Describing a large fireworks extravaganza elsewhere in Mexico, travel writer and folklorist Frances Toor writes, "The most beautiful and intricate of the fireworks pieces are the castles. They are about a hundred feet high, made in sections to represent saints, crowns, crosses, flowers, birds and other forms. Each section goes off separately, the whole taking from twenty minutes to a half hour and ending in a shower of dazzling light. There are also daylight castles, with humorous figures of animals and dolls that embrace and dance while the fireworks go off."[28] Toor's focus on the brilliant visual effect of these displays provides an exciting picture. At the same time, however, one can also imagine the dazzling sound and swirling, smoky smells they must have generated. Clear in each of these examples is the close connection between the use of pyrotechnics and various civic and religious outdoor celebrations.

In addition to these sanctioned sensual displays, Mexicans have also long indulged in a more informal deployment of pyrotechnics. The use of fireworks may constitute a "celebration of power" by an individual or small group within a larger community context. The deployable sights, sounds, and smells that characterize fireworks can similarly be used not only to engage in minor public transgressions but also to articulate a challenge, however elusive and temporary, to local authority. A few examples from Veracruz during the early 1920s will serve to illustrate this point.

Pyrotechnic Protests

In late April 1922—only a few years after the most violent years of the Mexican Revolution had passed—U.S. Department of State chargé d'affaires in Mexico City George Summerlin informed officials in Washington, DC, about activities planned for May 1, International Workers' Day. In his report, Summerlin quotes a broadsheet circulated by the Federation of Workmen's Syndicates of the Federal District on the international day of observance that reads:

> Fellow Workers:
>
> The First of May, which our enemies attempt to make appear as "The Labor Holiday," is not a festive day, but a date of mourning and of protest which workmen, now united, observe in order to demonstrate to the entire world that organized labor has not forgotten the assassinations which took place in 1886 in Chicago, Illinois.[29]

Responding to the federation's call, thousands of Mexico City residents joined in the 1922 May Day celebration with enthusiastic determination. Rallies held that day in the capital and other Mexican cities—including Puebla, Guadalajara, Jalapa, Colima, Pachuca, Chihuahua, and elsewhere—resembled, in certain ways, other gatherings throughout the Americas and Europe.

That same day in Veracruz, local government officials watched as red and black flags flew outside various labor union headquarters. Early that morning, members of the Revolutionary Syndicate of Tenants, led by anarchist Herón Proal, paraded south through the city to an area on the outskirts of town. Under the hot tropical sun, Proal and his entourage arrived at the site with their banners and flags. Once assembled, tenants took part in a ceremony that dedicated "the cornerstone" of a soon to be constructed building located in an area they decided would from that point on be known as the "communist neighborhood" (*colonia comunista*).

In the afternoon, residents set off firecrackers outside the headquarters of the local labor hall (Cámara de Trabajo) as workers, carrying banners of their respective organizations, assembled for a march through the city streets. Later, hundreds gathered in the city's Juárez Park where they listened to a number of prolabor speeches before continuing their celebration long into the night.[30] Extremely active in public affairs, the protest repertoire of the renters' movement included street demonstrations, parades, and direct action during their nearly decadelong rent protest in 1920s Veracruz.[31] Their choice of pyrotechnics, like those of other Mexican communities as a whole, clearly represented a statement about power in city as well as in state and national politics. A few examples will suffice.

After a legislative session in early January 1923 that put the final touches on a state housing reform law, tenants in the port of Veracruz gathered in the city's main plaza. Amid a sea of tenant syndicate banners, they shot off firecrackers before exuberantly parading, singing, and chanting through the streets.[32] A few months later, an amnesty issued by Veracruz governor Adalberto Tejeda freed approximately ninety incarcerated members of the Veracruz Revolutionary Syndicate from the Allende jail in the port. On the morning of May 11, 1923, sympathetic residents adorned their houses with banners and signs in anticipation of the prisoners' release. Gathered that afternoon outside the jail, well-wishers greeted their *compañeros* with firecrackers, jubilant cheering, and singing of revolutionary songs. Later that night, tenants organized a big rally to mark the occasion and renew their commitment to the renters' cause.[33]

In July of that same year, people from around the state gathered for a tenant convention in Veracruz. Marking the first anniversary of a deadly confrontation between federal troops and militant renters, Herón Proal presided over two days of meetings and strategizing. With the well-known anarchist Enrique Flores Magón in attendance, sympathizers gathered on the night of July 6 to celebrate the achievements of the movement and to mourn its losses. Once again, tenants articulated their solidarity with a repertoire that included fireworks, singing, chanting, and the occasional firing of pistols into the air. On this occasion, renters assaulted two alleged foreign-owned (Spanish) guesthouses with sticks, clubs, rocks, knives, and pistols. In one of the guesthouses, protesters seized the building and then hung syndicate banners from the upstairs windows. Seeing this, the crowd below reacted with glee and set off several rounds of firecrackers.[34] This same kind of antiforeign-motivated action had, in fact, occurred a few weeks before when tenants from another *pensión* had informed the Revolutionary Syndicate of their desire to quit paying rent. When union members visited the renters just before one of the nightly open-air meetings in a local park, the guesthouse residents hung red and black strike banners from their windows. Again, firecrackers played a part in acknowledging the bold move on the part of those who had decided to join the movement.[35]

Of course, these confrontations and other celebratory acts that included the use of pyrotechnics by tenant protesters in Veracruz did not go unnoticed by local authorities. At one point, just after officials had jailed Herón Proal, the editors of the local Veracruz paper *El Dictamen* issued a critical commentary on one of the most militant organizers of the Revolutionary Syndicate: María Luisa Marín. In an attack, they wrote

> Herón Proal [has] sent his woman, María Luisa Marín [to take] his place. [Since then, Marín has] . . . brought new energies and enthusiasms to the tenant cause. With equal vigor [she has] directed the [Syndicate's] business and, as in the past, collected dues that have made the protest such a prosperous enterprise for some time. María Luisa, as Proal has said, is an "intelligent" woman and one need only spend a short time here to become familiar with her activities: agitation in the patios, aggressive commentaries against the authorities, firecrackers and a full range of other gestures that usually culminate in the tumultuous public demonstrations that are by now well known and recalled with horror by the long suffering residents of this city.[36]

Clearly, the editors of *El Dictamen*, along with no small number of other Veracruz residents, had tired of not only the nonpayment of rents but also the regular confrontations, marches, manifestations, direct actions, and all-around fireworks-fueled agitprop instigated by the tenant strikers.

Adding this to our discussion, one can note that both official and informal uses of pyrotechnics are related to the larger question of local power and the making and remaking of social order. Here, Brandes's apt term *celebration of power* might also be further qualified by asking exactly whose power is being celebrated—and perhaps temporarily challenged—and why. It seems that, given the fact that so-called subaltern groups such as the Revolutionary Syndicate of Tenants can also articulate their own identity and power(however minor it might be) through pyrotechnic displays, we ought to amend both Brandes's and García Canclini's somewhat static assumptions to allow for the fact that unofficial groups can also make their own "celebrations." In so doing, they may bring into question the assumption that the status quo will be restored after the event. Having briefly considered both official and unofficial uses of fireworks in Veracruz history, let us now turn to the annual celebration of Carnival.

Carnival Sights and Sounds

According to the Christian calendar, Carnival marks an uproarious time of feasting and festivity before the advent of Lent. It is a presumed "world turned upside down" as social hierarchies are mockingly inverted, social decorum is made the subject of satire, copious amounts of food and drink are consumed, and sexual licentiousness is tolerated.

There are countless Carnival celebrations throughout Mexico.[37] In Veracruz, the pre-Lenten festival has been observed since the colonial period. Today, neighborhood groups (*comparsas*) fashion costumes and prepare their dance steps well in advance of the early spring ritual. As the official opening day of Carnival approaches, float makers work around the clock in warehouses and garages as they put the finishing touches on their commissioned works. At the same time, area hotel managers, restaurateurs, retailers, and Carnival organizers all anticipate the huge influx of visitors who come from neighboring towns and more distant cities.[38]

Documenting fireworks usage throughout the history of the Veracruz Carnival, although widespread, is difficult. No doubt part of colonial and early nineteenth-century merrymaking, official regulation of the festival beginning in 1867 attempted to keep control over potentially dangerous outbursts of violence, crime, and other, presumed antisocial behavior. Although not explicitly mentioned in the new law at the time, unofficial pyrotechnic practice may nevertheless have also become increasingly taboo. Pressure on the part of government authorities probably did little to diminish public enthusiasm for fireworks.[39]

Colleagues in the port tell me that firecrackers and larger pyrotechnics continued to be a regular part of the Carnival celebration after city boosters revived the celebration in 1925 after several years of nonobservance during the late nineteenth century and revolutionary years.[40] One person remembered festival processions headed by individuals who emulated small bulls (*toritos*) and carried a structure, strapped on their heads, that held fireworks and shot sparks and smoke.[41]

In the 1933 Mexican film *La mujer del puerto,* one can gain a sense of how fireworks were used in the celebration of Carnival. In a number of scenes, director Arcady Boytler sets his actors in a local Veracruz context, featuring an assortment of large pyrotechnics (various castillos) illuminating the background. One particularly dramatic portion of the film juxtaposes the funeral procession of Rosario's (played by Andrea Palma) father with the opening of Carnival and the destruction of Mal Humor, whose burning initiates the festival. Here, as Rosario mourns the loss of the family patriarch, rowdy revelers surround the coffin and gleefully throw confetti in what becomes a grotesque, chaotic display. Although the raucous sound and pungent smell of fireworks is not included in Boytler's creation, it takes little to imagine the powerful resonance of pyrotechnics as part of this Carnival drama.

During the modern celebration, an assemblage of police vehicles, percussion groups, dance ensembles, and floats make their way through the central city streets to the main plaza. In fact, not one but two different routes set the stage for Carnival parades during the festival. The aforementioned first and most historic circuit features the early *papaquis* processions and begins in the northeast corner of the historical downtown at the corner of 5 de Mayo and Montesinos near the former offices of the powerful railroad workers' union. This route then runs south along 5 de Mayo to Rayón and then back to Lerdo and then to the west side of the Plaza de Armas along spectator-packed Independence Avenue. Once in the central square, those in the procession make their way on foot to the festival stage that faces the local government buildings on the east side.

Prior to 1945, when electric lights on various floats allowed for evening circulation, daytime parades each year traveled this center-city circuit and, in so doing, announced to all the coming of Carnival. Then, as now, the first overture took place on Tuesday the week before Ash Wednesday and served as an invitation to all residents to come and join in the fun. The official opening ceremony of the festival begins with the burning of Mal Humor in front of a massive throng of spectators.

Mal Humor is an effigy figure understood to represent whatever negative force is ailing people and society at the time. To prepare for Mal Humor's destruction by fire, Carnival organizers build a huge statue largely out of wood, cardboard, and papier-mâché. They often fashion Mal Humor as an unpopular politician, kidnapper, or other social miscreant. Just before the start of Carnival, the sacrificial victim is set in the middle of the plaza. Then, after thousands have gathered on Tuesday evening, the official opening ceremony begins. A master of ceremonies selected for Carnival issues a series of pronouncements about the coming *alegría* (happiness or joy) to be symbolized with the ritual elimination of Mal Humor. A moment of collective liberation comes when organizers light a fire to the effigy, which is then subsequently engulfed in a funeral pyre. Torched and quickly reduced to smoldering ashes, it is publicly decreed that "Mal Humor is dead and now let us all enjoy Carnival."

After a series of nighttime processions following the downtown route not only on Tuesday but also on Wednesday, Thursday, and Friday nights (each corresponding to a separate coronation of Carnival royalty), the parading then moves to an eight-kilometer route that stretches south from the Malecón along the waterfront boulevard Manual Avila Camacho toward the neighboring town of Boca del Río. Because of the growing popularity of the festival since 1985, the Carnival committee oversees the Saturday through Tuesday night parades across this larger geography.

Starting just across from a yacht club and heading all the way south to a major corporate hotel zone just north of Boca del Río, the boulevard is lined with grandstands on both sides. Punctuating the long span of spectator structures on either side of the route are occasional metal towers that frame small stages equipped with powerful sound systems for DJs and dancers or local radio stations as they entertain the crowd before the arrival of the massive parade. After much anticipation, the procession is headed by a line of police vehicles with flashing lights and wailing sirens that clear the route. Carnival parades, though different each year, are generally composed of military bands dressed in white uniforms, a handful of samba schools, various baton twirling academies, and a vast throng of some forty comparsas and floats populated by costumed performers, celebrities, and assorted dignitaries. Constructed atop long, rectangular tractor trailers, many of these comparsas sport sound systems with massive stacks of speakers, behind which the troupes dance.

Taking in the spectacle from behind the heavily fenced-in grandstands, spectators cheer while they party with friends and family. Following the final boulevard parade on the Tuesday night (Shrove Tuesday) before Ash Wednesday, the city streets are nearly abandoned as revelers sleep off the cumulative impact of more than a week of Carnival enthusiasm. On Wednesday, all that remains is one last parade through the city center and the burning and subsequent burial of Juan Carnival. Traditionally, Juan Carnival is known to be the son of Rey Momo—the true father of Carnival. In a manner parallel to the Christian sacrificial ritual, Juan Carnival is put to death so that he—in a kind of mock conception of Christ's resurrection—may "rise again" the following year.[42]

When the first renewed celebration took place in 1925 after several years of official nonobservance, Juan Carnival was put to death on Shrove Tuesday. That night, a rowdy, alcohol-soaked crowd of approximately one thousand revelers paraded around the city's central district, singing and setting off firecrackers as a way to announce the impending end of the pre-Lenten festival. A small effigy of Juan Carnival was carried by members of the railroad union. Once they arrived in the Plaza de Armas, they set Juan Carnival afire and watched him burn while shouting praises in his honor and shooting off more firecrackers.[43] With the Carnival king reduced to ashes, everyone knew the celebration had ended and a forty-day season of self-sacrifice had arrived.

During contemporary observances in Veracruz, Shrove Tuesday is designated as the final night of partying as the Carnival queen and her court bid goodbye, and the celebration extends long into the night. The funerary rite for Juan Carnival takes place the following evening on Ash Wednesday, when there is no actual burning of his effigy; rather, a large coffin is brought out on a stage in the main plaza, and his death is (mockingly) mourned by a theater troupe of dancers and actors along with the Carnival court. Following the choreographed closing ceremony, a band plays and the public is encouraged to dance and enjoy the evening.

Today, the use of fireworks in Veracruz seems to have diminished significantly, and there are apparently fewer producers of large pyrotechnics in the area. It is said by locals that people tend to buy in Puebla or other places and then bring the fireworks to Veracruz to sell. In the place of private deployment, municipalities have institutionalized the opening and closing ceremonies of Carnival and significantly regulated pyrotechnic display.[44] Whatever the contemporary attitude may be, there is little doubt, despite the relatively slim body of contemporary available evidence, that fireworks and related ritual practices such as effigy burnings during Carnival have played an important part in the cultural life of the city.

Candelaria: Honoring the Virgin, Marking Inclusivity

Approximately one hundred kilometers south of Veracruz, in the charming riverside town of Tlacotalpan, residents and hundreds of visitors gather every year in late January and early February to honor their patron saint: the Virgin of Candelaria. Fiesta de la Candelaria is (at the least) a seventy-year-old festival during which pyrotechnics are deployed to mark festival time, chase off evil spirits, and celebrate local power.[45]

As Candelaria takes place in late January and early February, it runs concurrent with the annual Veracruz regional *son jarocho* folk music festival known as the Encuentro Nacional de Jaraneros y Decimistas.[46] Extending throughout the small town geography from the Papoalapan riverfront to the main plaza Zaragoza (also known as the Zócalo) and into a few other key gathering places—all well within walking distance—the resulting atmosphere in the relatively small festival space is a sumptuous mix of traditional music, civic celebration, and religious veneration.

In private kitchens, residents prepare savory, traditional cuisine in anticipation of the festival. Fresh, "Veracruz-styled" fish (often red snapper) with tomato, olive, garlic, chili pepper, and onion is featured along with rice in fish broth (*arroz a la tumbada*) and special sausage (*loganiza*) as mainstays. Various sweets include white gorditas, stuffed oranges (*naranjas rellanas*), and the caramelized milk treat *dulce de leche*. With the smell of these and other delicious foods wafting out of windows and into the streets as cooks go about their business, the celebration begins as artisans from far and wide make their way to Tlacotalpan where they sell their wares in temporary markets (*tianguis*).

In time, savory flavors wafting through the air combine with the bustle of informal commerce and the sound of harps and various guitars (typically the smaller, homemade *requintos* and *jaranas*). As the music festival shifts into gear, one hears foot stomping *zapateado* dance rhythms resonating from wooden stages and across much of the town. Taken together, this is the rich sensory backdrop from which the festival of Candelaria begins.

In contrast to the much more highly developed tourist infrastructure in neighboring Veracruz, Tlacotalpan has few actual hotels—a situation that forces many overnight visitors to find accommodation in private homes or pitch a tent and sleep out of doors. Far from putting a damper on things, however, the resulting effect is one that lends itself to all-night music jams, dancing, and all-around congenial socializing.[47] For the 2006 celebration, organizers set official events in motion with a cavalcade (dubbed Cabalgata) of local horses and riders on January 31. Dressed in the typical *jarocho* regional costume of white linen, red scarves, and straw hats, those on horseback are mostly young kids accompanied by their parents on foot.

Participants, well-wishers, and observers first gather in the town center as official opening pronouncements are made by local officials over loudspeakers set up on either side of an official viewing stand. Musicians, vendors, journalists, tourists, and residents mill about as emergency and police vehicles prepare for the parade. Once the event is declared officially under way, the Cabalgata methodically makes its way around the town. The sound of horses' hooves, cheers, and a recording of the Mexican national anthem inform—and ostensibly invite—all local residents to the festival.

The next morning, there is a modest running of the bulls (Corrido de Toros) where young men, however unfortunately, taunt the animals in some supposed testament to their bravado. Daily regattas on the nearby Papaloapan River, dancing and music events (fandangos), socializing, shopping, drinking, and eating keep things lively throughout the day. Later that night, a street parade known as the Mojiganga takes place. It is a raucous affair with giant papier-mâché figures, costumed dancers, flaming torches, music, and fireworks.

The Mojiganga: Sound and Vision

The term *Mojiganga* generally denotes a form of street theater that dates back to early modern Spain and probably well before.[48] In the context of Candelaria, Mojiganga is a boisterous parade that occurs the night before the crowning Virgin of Candelaria river event (Paseo de la Virgen).

Beginning around 8:00 in the evening, approximately thirty (mostly younger) participants assemble in the northwest corner of the main plaza. Some don costumes that make them appear as bulls, whereas others wear papier-mâché boat constructions painted in bright, pastel colors. The Mojiganga figures themselves appear as giant heads attached to six- or seven-foot pikes and serve to illustrate various "negative" forces being driven out of town.[49] Rounding out the parade are usually an assortment of people wearing red T-shirts and sporting papier-mâché fish, ducks, smiley-faced suns, beetle-shell print umbrellas, banners, streamers, flags, and, of course, the proverbial dark, skeletal figure of death (*la muerte*).

With the procession further animated by celestial images set atop extended wooden poles, the Mojiganga is intended, as historian Ricardo Pérez Montfort observes, "to rid the town of evil and sin" the night before the Virgin is honored.[50] With the loud and colorful character of these images, townsfolk are kept up to date on the progression of the festival as the honoring of the Virgin draws ever near. Beginning with dramatic, flaming gas torches that are lit by participants, the procession first makes its rounds in the Tlacotalpan Zócalo. Parading around the plaza perimeter by firelight, much shouting, chanting, and dancing attract attention. Firecrackers and bottle rockets are set off every few seconds. At the end of the phalanx, trumpet and tenor saxophone players set a rhythmic call and response pattern that accompanies the parade as it moves beyond the city center and out into the surrounding neighborhoods. The raucous Mojiganga advances slowly as it is led by a municipal pickup truck flashing its lights and a small car with speakers mounted atop playing recorded music. Youthful participants walk along with fiery torches and papier-mâché figures. Others move from side to side in bull and boat costumes, yelling "woo hoo," "yi, yi, yah," and other enthusiastic bits. The saxophone and trumpet players continue apace with their spontaneous back-and-forth phrasing.

Pyrotechnics, ranging from small "ladyfinger" noisemakers to bottle rockets and cherry bombs, punctuate the procession with their arrhythmic explosions. Their use adds tension and excitement to the parade. Surprise is a key experiential element, since only one or two individuals know exactly where and when any given explosion will occur. Fireworks can both dazzle and delight, but they can also frighten, shock, and intimidate spectators. As intended, this auspicious display of sight, smell, and sound brings many people out of their houses as they smile, applaud, whistle, and shout. The early evening spectacle is largely understood as a joyous and sensuous invitation. It is a ritual performance that engenders an inclusive, community ethos. Thanks to the distinctive deployment of popular music and pyrotechnics, the Mojiganga appropriately paves the way for the more somber Paseo de la Virgen the following day.

The Final Paseo

The Virgin of Candelaria procession is the main event of the festival. Cloaked in a white-and-gold-trimmed cape and gown, the honored figure is a female mannequin that appears young with light skin color; a long blond wig; and a far-away, statuesque gaze. From her permanent home inside the Tlacotalpan central cathedral, the Virgin stands on a massive, decorated wood platform as she is carried out by nearly forty middle-aged men. Leading the procession is the archbishop of Veracruz and other leading clergy members (many from the Cofradía de Nuestra Señora del Carmen) who direct the procession a short way through the town streets to the Papaloapan River, where they will then board a waiting ferry and travel upriver for about an hour, accompanied by a slew of decorated, smaller watercraft.[51] Eventually, back on shore, the Virgin is carried back and reinstalled in the cathedral for another year. With this, the people of Tlacotalpan, as well as the many visitors to the picturesque river town, understand that their patron saint has been paid her rightful due. In return, many hope she will protect and watch over them.

During Candelaria, there are public fireworks displays nearly every night. Here again, the overall effect produced among the spectators is one of delight and awe. These large, commercial pyrotechnics render brilliant, colorful displays of light, while, at the same time, they punctuate the night air with crackling sounds, loud reports, whistling shrieks, and thundering, sonic booms. In 2010, the evening following the procession of the Virgin was dedicated to fireworks accompanied by music.

Pyrotechnics: Why Bother?

People in Veracruz—like so many others in Mexico and around the world—have used pyrotechnics in their celebrations of religious and civic festivals for many years. With a packed holiday schedule filled with observances of Three Kings' Day, Candelaria, Carnival, Semana Santa, El Día de los Novios y de la Amistad, El Día de la Madre, El Día del Niño, Fiestas Patrias, El Día de la Raza, Día de Los Muertos, La Guadalupana, and a full range of local saints' days, there is virtually not a month that goes by without a major festival somewhere in the state.

One might ask: why all the effort and expense? Certainly, there are clear social reasons for these fireworks displays. In the midst of all the merry-making and socializing, a certain general mood is set. Pyrotechnics—powerful, commanding, and easily accessible—are deployed to create a shared experience. They often are used to mark ritual time, entice people, and symbolically clear the air of certain negative forces so celebrations can proceed. Although obnoxious, frightening, or just downright annoying to some, pyrotechnics are mostly meant to be fun. They temporarily disturb while also dazzling us with their brilliance, noise, and smell. If, as Brandes writes, "fireworks bear anthropological attention for their political meaning," we can appreciate that fireworks help us understand ways individuals within communities construct social and cultural meaning and how they go about envisioning themselves as part of the larger social order.[52]

POSTSCRIPT
SOUND REPRESENTATION

Nation, Translation, Memory

Michele Hilmes

THERE IS A space between the essential ephemerality of a sonic utterance and the process through which it is preserved and transmitted to others that has been taken up under the name of *sound studies,* an emergent category of scholarship to which this volume generously contributes and expands. We often think of an utterance as composed solely of vocalized words, but words form only a part of the types of utterances considered by scholars of sound. Much in the domain of sound eschews words altogether in favor of that special category we classify as music, or the wider range of sounds, ambient or constructed, that do the work of conveying place, position, action, emotion, and identity. Nevertheless, James Lastra reminds us that, far from possessing "natural" meaning, all sonic utterances are constructed representations that result from "an interlocking set of diverse practices" and not a simple "act of pure inscription."[1] Whether performed live (in festivals or on stage), transmitted simultaneously (via radio or telephone), or reproduced (via recording or writing), sounds in their creation and in their context are *representations:* the product of a specific communication situation, layered with meaning.

Thinking of sound as representation rather than as the unproblematic manifestation of physical events or verbal communication opens up a realm of analysis in which it is imperative to understand the specific cultural context within which aural meaning is made. One key context is that of *nation.* We have paid close attention to national literature, art, theater, dance, and music, but as Alejandra Bronfman and Andrew Grant Wood point out in their introduction to this book, national soundscapes have received far less sustained analysis. This volume serves as a reminder that there are many good reasons to study sound as a national phenomenon. First, sonic utterances more often than not are represented in a national language, with its subtle shifts in meaning captured in dialect, pronunciation, and word choice; we see this clearly in Christine Ehrick's chapter on radio in Argentina, where the work of sound in setting and transgressing the conventions of gender and sexuality is analyzed within the context of a particular period of national cultural history. Equally important is the fact that the representation, transmission, and reception of sonic utterances have been strongly structured by the nation, across the twentieth century and into the twenty-first. This occurs not only in terms of access to technology but also in the establishment of complex systems of sound production and distribution, most significantly through radio, that determine who may be heard and who may listen—and what they may hear, in both public and private spaces.

Radio in particular became the twentieth century's primary medium of national communication and definition, through which much of its culture was expressed. Such circuits of sound map closely onto political spheres, so that even though radio is ideally suited to transgressing boundaries and defying borders, nations around the world placed it under tighter control, via state broadcasters and state regulation, than any other modern medium. In the words of Rudolf Arnheim, one of the medium's earliest theorists, radio "insists on the unity of national culture and makes for centralization, collectivism and standardization."[2] Nationalized technological systems such as radio, the telephone, and the telegraph became primary sites for production and circulation of the nation's voice. Alejandra Bronfman's chapter shows how layers of practice, built up around institutionalized sound circuits, provided for multiple and sometimes conflicting sites of control and regulation. Radio, in particular, thanks to its border-crossing abilities, also functioned as a way for nations to speak to and about each other, as Gisela Cramer traces in her chapter on U.S. broadcasts to Latin America during the 1930s and 1940s. Other important locations of representations of sound, such as festivals, carnivals, parades, and demonstrations that reflect the local and regional cultures of the nation, also found their place on radio—as they do in this book.

Within the nation, those sites of utterance outside the dominant language and the dominant system are frequently neglected, as in the case of Spanish-language radio in the United States or stations broadcasting in Native American languages. In Canada, the scholarly literature on French-language broadcasting remains largely uncited by scholars working in English, and vice versa. Even though nations such as Canada, Britain, Australia, and the United States share a common language—as do the majority of Caribbean and Central and South American nations—only recently has academic study begun to break down the remnants of national systems to consider sonic utterance across boundaries as a transnational phenomenon. Work that crosses both national and linguistic borders is so rare as to be exceptional. This volume presents an opening up of the sonic landscape of Latin America and the Caribbean to Anglophone scholars, bringing disparate regions and nations into convergence across a wide range of periods and locations. This marks an important moment in sound studies, pointing the way toward an understanding of sonic representation as both a national and transnational set of concerns.

As always, such expansion requires a process of translation, in both a literal and symbolic sense, and further in terms with which we are only slowly coming to grips in this era of digital media. Most obviously, the contributors to this volume perform the service of literally translating utterances that occur in the Spanish or Portuguese languages for circulation in English-based scholarship. To do this, they employ not only linguistic skills but also knowledge of other social and historical contexts in which such utterances are embedded. Often, the sources used to pursue their research are not direct reproductions of sound as it was created in the moment—what we simply call "recordings"—but traces of the experience of sound translated into writing and represented in lasting but secondary form in documents, reports, transcripts, and literature, as is shown particularly clearly in Fernando de Sousa Rocha's chapter on sound's representation in turn-of-the-twentieth-century Brazilian poetry and literature.

This process of translation from the ephemerality of the sonic event to the permanence of some other medium can only give us indirect access to the experience of hearing it as it happened.

The role of translation is particularly acute when dealing with traces of sound from the past, now retrieved and interpreted from the land of the present. Sound has never had the same kind of fixed material continuity as a written record or as a work of visual expression—those forms that present themselves to the eye and have a palpable presence. A sonic utterance has the characteristics of a performance, an event that takes place over time and, when it ends, effectively ceases to exist. Recordings can represent such a performance, but they are subject to the variables not only of perception but also of technological parameters that materially change the nature of the event. Every recording brings with it its own process of representation, from selection of the recordable to the specific conditions of its creation, its preservation, and its later retrieval by historians. At any of these moments, as Michel-Rolph Trouillot reminds us, history can be silenced: a metaphor especially appropriate for sound culture. At every stage of historical production—fact creation, fact assembly, fact retrieval, and retroactive significance[3]—sound evades the historical record. In fact, according to Jonathan Sterne, "sound recording did as much to promote ephemerality as it did to promote permanence in auditory life,"[4] since it helped to make recorded sound artifacts both ubiquitous and easily disposable.

Ironically, perhaps the need for an awareness of the representative nature of sound and its dependence on context for translation has been made even greater by the technology that also allows us access to the world of sound across all manner of boundaries, including past and present: digital reproduction. As a quick Google search can demonstrate, the term *sound representation* has in fact been appropriated by the world of computer programming specialists and is commonly used to refer to the translation into modified and abstracted forms that occurs when sound is digitized. Such sound, when it reaches our ears, has gone through a process of streamlining and reduction in density that enables it to be transmitted as a series of zeros and ones, broken into pieces to be reassembled at the site of reception. As we know, digitization also allows for manipulation, recombination, and mashing together of sound in ways never dreamed of by earlier artists and technicians with their aspirations toward "fidelity." Digital reproduction preserves and makes accessible traces of sound history to a magnitude never before possible, but equally it strips them of context, complexity, and depth, or it substitutes contexts that provide new meanings but work to obscure others.

It is interesting that, of the seven chapters in this book, only one deals with recorded sound per se, and that one, by Alejandro L. Madrid, specifically calls attention to the deconstruction and reconstitution of the sonic utterance by a variety of forces, political, economic, and technological. Most of the others rely on the dominant historical record of sound, as mentioned above—its capture in writing—bringing once again to the fore the problematic of memory when it comes to the ephemeral sonic event. Gonzalo Araoz specifically invokes the work of sound memory, hearing carnival music in his head in a distant time and space from the events that produced it, and reflecting on what that means. Andrew Grant Wood's chapter, provocatively, relies on the recounting of sounds almost impossible to capture or notate, in fact notable precisely for their ability to violate the sonic mainstream, to startle, and to transgress.

Thus, memory is the final task of sound scholarship: to invoke a memory of never entirely recuperable sonic events as they occurred, to translate them from that point of occurrence and to represent them as the work of a context in which nation, translation, and memory play crucial parts. Memory is a mental process, a product of imagination that in many ways reproduces the process by which sound takes on meaning; sound divorced from the "fixing" qualities of the visual remains ambiguous, liminal, contingent, and open to a range of interpretations and transgressions. We imagine sounds as we imagine the communities that produced them. If we could hear the sonic utterances discussed by these authors—had they been preserved as recordings, were we able to access them, should they be included in this printed format—how much would our understandings be altered? Most likely, I surmise, very little—we would still need the translation and the memory work that their analysis provides. How fortunate to have the contribution that these essays make to our ongoing study of world sound cultures.

NOTES

Introduction: Media, Sound, and Culture

Epigraphs: Elvis Presley, "Seeing Is Believing," words and music by Red West and Glenn Spreen, recorded on May 19, 1971, in Nashville, on *He Touched,* RCA Records; Jacques Attali, *Noise: The Political Economy of Music* (Minneapolis: University of Minnesota Press, 1986), 3. Originally published in French as *Bruits: Essai sur l'économie politique de la musique* (Paris: Presses Universitaires de France, 1977).

1. Attali, *Noise.*
2. Greg Milner, *Perfecting Sound Forever: An Aural History of Recorded Music* (New York: Faber and Faber, 2009), 15.
3. R. Murray Schafer, *The Tuning of the World* (Philadelphia: University of Pennsylvania Press, 1981); Alain Corbin, *Village Bells: Sound and Meaning in the 19th century French Countryside* (New York: Columbia University Press, 1998); David Cressy, *Bonfires and Bells: National Memory and the Protestant Calendar in Elizabethan and Stuart England* (London: Weidenfeld & Nicolson, 1989).

4. Leigh Eric Schmidt, *Hearing Things: Religion, Illusion, and the American Enlightenment* (Cambridge, MA: Harvard University Press, 2000); Richard Cullen Rath, *How Early America Sounded* (Ithaca, NY: Cornell University Press, 2004); Mark Smith, *Listening to Nineteenth-Century America* (Chapel Hill: University of North Carolina Press, 2001).

5. Jonathan Sterne, *The Audible Past: Cultural Origins of Sound Reproduction* (Durham, NC: Duke University Press, 2003); Emily Thompson, *The Soundscape of Modernity: Architectural Acoustics and the Culture of Listening in America, 1900–1933* (Cambridge, MA: MIT Press, 2002).

6. Charles Hirschkind, *The Ethical Soundscape: Cassette Sermons and Islamic Counterpublics* (New York: Columbia University Press, 2006); Kevin Birth, *Bacchanalian Sentiments: Musical Experiences and Political Counterpoints in Trinidad* (Durham, NC: Duke University Press, 2008); Michael Veal, *Dub: Soundscapes and Shattered Songs in Jamaican Reggae* (Middletown, CT: Wesleyan University Press, 2007).

7. Reynaldo González, *Llorar es un placer* (Havana: Editorial Letras Cubanas, 2002); Inés Cornejo Portugal, *Apuntes para una historia de la radio indigenista en México* (México: Editorial Manuel Buendia, 2002); Rubén Gallo, *Mexican Modernity: The Avant-Garde and the Technological Revolution* (Cambridge, MA: MIT Press, 2005); Guillermo Mastrini, ed, *Mucho ruido, pocas leyes: Economía y políticas de comunicación en la Argentina (1920–2007)* (Buenos Aires: La Crujía Ediciones, 2009).

8. Bryan McCann, *Hello, Hello Brazil: Popular Music and the Making of Modern Brazil* (Durham, NC: Duke University Press, 2004); Sergio Arribá, "El Peronismo y la Política de Radiodifusión (1946–1955)" in Mastrini, *Mucho ruido, pocas leyes*.

9. Oscar Luis López, *La radio en Cuba* (Havana: Editorial Letras Cubanas, 1998); Joy Hayes, *Radio Nation: Communication, Popular Culture and Nationalism in Mexico, 1920–1950* (Tucson: University of Arizona Press, 2000); Robert Claxton, *From Parsifal to Perón: Early Radio in Argentina, 1920–1944* (Gainesville: University Press of Florida, 2007).

10. We are also inspired by Michele Hilmes, who has argued that sound studies needs to expand beyond North America and Europe, lest those narratives come to be read as universals. See Michele Hilmes, "Is there a Field Called Sound Culture Studies? And Does it Matter?"*American Quarterly* 57, no. 1 (2005): 249–59.

11. See, among others, Peter Wade, *Music, Race and Nation: Música Tropical in Colombia* (Chicago: University of Chicago Press, 2000); Gage Averill, *A Day for the Hunter, A Day for the Prey: Popular Music and Power in Haiti* (Chicago:

University of Chicago Press, 1997); Deborah Pacini Hernández, *Bachata: A Social History of Dominican Music* (Philadelphia: Temple University Press, 1997); Frances Aparicio, *Listening to Salsa: Gender, Latin Popular Music and Puerto Rican Cultures* (Middletown, CT: Wesleyan University Press, 1998); Margaret Dorsey, *Pachangas: Borderlands Music, U.S. Politics and Transnational Marketing* (Austin: University of Texas Press, 2006); Ned Sublette, *Cuba and Its Music: From the First Drums to the Mambo* (Chicago: Chicago Review Press, 2007); Chris McGowan and Ricardo Pessanha, *The Brazilian Sound: Samba, Bossa Nova and the Popular Music of Brazil* (Philadelphia: Temple University Press, 2008); Jocelyne Guilbault, *Governing Sound: The Cultural Politics of Trinidad's Carnival Musics* (Chicago: University of Chicago Press, 2007).

12. Jesus Martín-Barbero, *Communication, Culture and Hegemony* (London: Sage Publications, 1998).

13. Lisa Gitelman, *Always Already New: Media, History, and the Data of Culture* (Cambridge, MA: MIT Press, 2006).

14. Roland Barthes, "The Grain of the Voice," in *Image, Music, Text* (New York: Noonday Press, 1977), 179–89.

1. Recovering Voices: The Popular Music Ear in Late Nineteenth- and Early Twentieth-Century Brazil

Epigraph: Mia Couto, "O apocalipse privado do tio Geguê," in *Cada homem é uma raça* (Lisbon: Caminho, 1990), 32. I translate the passage in the following manner: "How could that voice happen? She was nobody and could only make use of silences." In David Brookshaw's translation, the same passage reads: "How could she speak like that? She was no one, silence was her only tool" (Mia Couto, "The Private Apocalypse of Uncle Geguê," in *Every Man Is a Race,* trans. David Brookshaw [Oxford: Heinemann, 1994], 13).

1. R. Murray Schafer, *The Soundscape: Our Sonic Environment and the Tuning of the World* (Rochester, VT: Destiny Books, 1994).

2. Ricardo Palma, "Carta canta," in *Tradiciones peruanas completas* (Madrid: Aguilar, 1968), 146–48. English translations for Palma's text are taken from "A Letter Sings," *Peruvian Traditions,* trans. Helen Lane (Oxford: Oxford University Press, 2004), 89–93.

3. Avery F. Gordon, *Ghostly Matters: Haunting and the Sociological Imagination* (Minneapolis: University of Minnesota Press, 1997), 6.

4. Lima Barreto, *Triste fim de Policarpo Quaresma* (São Paulo: Ática, 1997).

5. Machado de Assis, "Um homem célebre," in *Várias histórias* (Rio de Janeiro: W. W. Jackson, 1970), 65–84. English translations for Machado de As-

sis's story are taken from "A Celebrity," in *The Devil's Church and Other Stories*, trans. Jack Schmitt and Lorie Ishimatsu (Austin: University of Texas Press, 1977), 107–15.

6. As Julio Ortega points out, the story of the stolen fruit is found in different Latin American regions, including the Caribbean islands and Brazil. See Julio Ortega, "Escritura colonial, lectura poscolonial: El sujeto trasatlántico," *Signos Literarios y Lingüísticos* 3, no. 1 (2001): 15–31.

7. Palma, "Carta canta," 147. The English translation reads: "The one who throws me out of my house and land I will throw out of this world" (Palma, "A Letter Sings," 91).

8. Palma, "A Letter Sings," 92.

9. Ortega, "Escritura colonial, lectura poscolonial," 27.

10. Barreto, *Triste fim de Policarpo Quaresma,* 85.

11. Ibid.

12. Ibid., 86.

13. Domingos Caldas Barbosa (c. 1740–1800) is responsible for popularizing the Brazilian modinha among Portuguese aristocrats. His poems, for which he composed both modinhas and *lundus*, were collected under the title *Viola de Lereno.* The first volume appeared in 1798, and the second appeared in 1825 in Brazil and 1826 in Portugal. He is, in this sense, Ricardo's fortunate forerunner, the fatherly voice that Ricardo, as a true heir, attempts to continue in early twentieth-century Brazil. In fact, Ricardo's full name—Ricardo Coração dos Outros (Ricardo Others' Hearts)—duplicates the singer-listener relationship that he identifies in Caldas Barbosa's (Lereno's) performances before Portuguese aristocrats. It thus constitutes one of the narrative constructs that function as a resonating box in which Ricardo wishes to hear his own authorial voice.

14. Castro Alves, "Vozes d'África," in *Poesia* (Rio de Janeiro: Agir, 1966), 87–92. English translations to Castro Alves's poem are mine.

15. Barreto, *Triste fim de Policarpo Quaresma,* 86.

16. Ibid.

17. "Isto é bom" and "Bolim Bolacho" ("Lundu do Baiano") are both found in music CD 1 that accompanies Humberto Franceschi's *A Casa Edison e seu tempo* (Rio de Janeiro: PETROBRÁS; Biscoito Fino, 2002).

18. For the characteristics of oral "textuality," see Walter J. Ong, *Orality and Literacy: The Technologizing of the Word* (London: Methuen, 1982).

19. All translations to song lyrics are mine.

20. In many cases, one may trace popular song verses back centuries, indicating that they put into play a detached voice, which the singer actualizes in

his or her performance. As José Ramos Tinhorão notes, the aforementioned verses from "Isto é bom" are found in the *Almocreve de petas*, a series of *feuilletons* by José Daniel Rodrigues da Costa (1757–1832), compiled in three volumes between 1817 and 1819 (Tinhorão, *O rasga: Uma dança negro-portuguesa* [São Paulo: Editora 34, 2006], 29–30). Tinhorão suggests that Xisto Bahia must have heard the stanza—"perhaps already transformed into 'popular motif'"— during the second half of the nineteenth century and "without hesitation, incorporated it to the lyrics of his *lundu*, without thinking twice" (Tinhorão, *O rasga*, 30; translations mine.).

21. For an insightful reading of Machado de Assis's story, see José Miguel Wisnik, "Machado maxixe: O caso Pestana," *Teresa* 4–5 (2004): 13–79.

22. Assis, "Um homem célebre," 67; Assis, "A Celebrity," 107, for the English translation.

23. Assis, "Um homem célebre," 68 (translation mine). In Schmitt and Ishimatsu's translation, this phrase is rendered as "the tune was on everybody's lips" (Assis, "A Celebrity," 108). However, it does not translate the subtleties of the original, such as the contrast between "consagração" and "assobio/cantarola" and the fact that the song and its author are conflated in this contrast. It is also important to note that "cantarola" entails a certain degree of unconsciousness. It is an unassuming, inattentive singing, without any purpose, as if the singing took place despite the singer.

24. Lúcio Rangel reprints in *Sambistas e chorões* an old newspaper article from his archives, in which Noel Rosa (1910–1937) describes his trajectory as a musician. Although Rangel is not certain whether Rosa himself wrote the article or if it is the result of an interview, the depiction of Rosa's relationship to his listeners and of the sonic effects his songs have on listeners is similar to those in Lima Barreto's and Machado de Assis's stories. After Rosa composes his first melody, which is positively received by friends and relatives, he feels that his future is clearer and that he is not "far from popularity, fame, and, in sum, glory." His objective was to see his music "popularized throughout the city, propagated by the most different voices, flourishing in anonymous whistling, in the neighborhood pianos and vitrolas." And he further imagines his prestige, once his songs achieved such prominence: he would be spotted by unknown people, who would say "That one over there is Noel!" or "Look, there's Noel!" Just like Pestana and Ricardo Coração dos Outros, Noel feels that, with his songs famous, he "had penetrated the city's heart; he comprehended the *carioca* sensibility and knew how to communicate with the people." However, he also senses that his "glory would only be definitive after [his] songs were perpetuated on records," suggesting that, for composers, sound record-

ing might function in the same manner that print technology did, regarding the survival of the name. Lúcio Rangel, *Sambistas e chorões: Aspectos e figuras da música popular brasileira* (São Paulo: Francisco Alves, 1962), 82–85; translations to Rangel's book are mine.

25. Assis, "Um homem célebre," 72; Assis, "A Celebrity," 109.

26. Assis, "Um homem célebre," 78; Assis, "A Celebrity," 112.

27. Assis, "Um homem célebre," 80; Assis, "A Celebrity," 113.

28. In the original Portuguese, "um grande Pestana invisível" (Assis, "Um homem célebre," 80), "grande" may translate both as "great" and "big." We may thus read the "irony and perversity" of the scene in the manner in which Pestana's greatness, as a famous composer but not an immortal one, is reaffirmed (ibid.; Assis, "A Celebrity," 113). The immense Pestana is an invigorated ghost who, after having been unsuccessfully shooed away, returns to claim his position, his greatness, and his listeners, despite the author-person's own desires. In fact, his detachment from the author-person is the most unrebuttable proof of the greatness of Pestana the polka composer.

29. Assis, "Um homem célebre," 71; Assis, "A Celebrity," 109.

30. Donga and Mauro de Almeida, "Pelo telefone," with Baiano (voice), Humberto Franceschi, *A Casa Edison e seu tempo* (Biscoito Fino, 2002), compact disc 2, first released in December, 1916.

31. Carlos Sandroni's *Feitiço decente: Transformações do samba no Rio de Janeiro, 1917–1933* (Rio de Janeiro: Zahar/Editora UFRJ, 2001) provides significant information on the issue. According to Mauro de Almeida, the composer of the lyrics for "Pelo telefone," the song's verses were taken from popular stanzas, and he confesses: "To the people their *rolinha* [the bird mentioned in the song], which is more theirs than mine" (quoted in Sandroni, *Feitiço decente,* 119; all translations to Sandroni's text are mine). However, Donga and Almeida registered the song at the National Library in Rio de Janeiro as being *their* composition. In retaliation, Tia Ciata, Sinhô, and other *sambistas*—who claimed that the song was a collective composition created at Tia Ciata's house— replied with a parodic stanza: "Tomara que tu apanhes / Pra não tornar fazer isso / Escrever o que é dos outros / Sem olhar o compromisso" (I hope they beat you up / So you won't do that again / To write down what belongs to others / Regardless of any commitment) (ibid.). What is meant here by commitment is not only an acknowledgment that "Pelo telefone" was a collective composition, but also recognition that, once the sambista signed the song as his, he problematized the ties that linked his voice to the detached, communal voice. As Sandroni points out, Donga transformed "something that, up to that moment, was restricted to a small community into a genre of popular song, in

the modern sense of the term, with an author, recording, access to the media, success before society as a whole" (ibid., 120). It is important here to notice that, in their parodic verses, the sambistas specifically say that Donga wrote the song down, as if implying that it was precisely the act of writing that produced an author for the samba, beyond the polyphony that one may find in songs from the early years of the twentieth century, including "Pelo telefone." Such a process, as Sandroni rightly points out, could not take place if Donga had not recurred to "the music score for piano, which was to be commercialized; the arrangement for a band; the printed lyrics, whose fixity transformed all subsequent improvisations into mere parodies; the recording" (ibid.). Moreover, as an embodiment of this bridge between oral and print cultures, "Pelo telefone" is also signed by Mauro de Almeida, who is associated at the same time with the world of music and that of letters. Almeida took part in Rio de Janeiro's Carnival *clubes* and was a journalist who also wrote theatrical plays.

32. Carmen Miranda, vocal performance of "Iaiá, ioiô," by Josué de Barros, on *Carmen Miranda*, RCA Victor/BMG 7432152774-2, 1998, compact disc 1, first released in February 1930.

33. Sandroni, *Feitiço decente*, 122.

34. Ibid., 125–27.

35. Noel Rosa, "Rapaz folgado," with Aracy de Almeida (voice) and Conjunto Regional RCA Victor, on *Noel Rosa por Mário Reis e Aracy de Almeida* (Revivendo, n.d.), recorded on April 28, 1938, and first released in October 1938. In this song—Rosa's famous response to "Lenço no pescoço," a song recorded that same year and in which Wilson Batista (1913–1968) praises the *malandro*—an idler who was closely linked to the world of samba—Rosa attempts to instruct the sambista-malandro: "With your crooked hat, you made a fool of yourself / From the police I want you to escape / Composing a *samba-canção* / I have already given you paper and pencil / Now you must find a love and a guitar." In his song, Batista states that the malandro is a "vadio" (idler) precisely because, when he was a child, he would compose samba-canções. Contrary to such a viewpoint, what Rosa expects from the sambista is that he should not give himself away to the police by the manner he wears his hat or because he composes sambas, but, rather, being a sambista should be a sign of distinction that would free sambistas from being stopped, and possibly arrested, by the police. Such evolution in the way society perceived the figure of the sambista was only possible if, as Rosa suggests, the composer carried paper and pencil in hand—if, in other words, he or she abandoned the world of oral dissemination of texts and entered that of letters. What such entrance also entails, however, is a specific use of one's body. Malandros should no longer drag

their clogs or *gingar* or swing their bodies in fights in which they would put their *navalha* (pocket knife) to use. Paper and pencil instead required a taming of the body—its immobilization—so that writing is produced.

36. Evan Eisenberg, *The Recording Angel: Music, Records and Culture from Aristotle to Zappa* (New Haven, CT: Yale University Press, 2005), 46.

37. Ibid., 47.

38. Ibid.

39. Raimundo Correia, "As pombas," in *Poesia* (Rio de Janeiro: Agir, 1958).

40. Carmen Miranda, vocal performance of "Triste jandaia," by Josué de Barros, on *Carmen Miranda*, RCA Victor/BMG 7432152774-2, 1998, compact disc 1, first released in January 1930.

41. Seu Jorge, vocal performance of "Pequinês e pitbull," by Gabriel Moura, Lulu Aranha, and Jovi Joviniano, *Carolina*, Mr. Bongo, n.d. *Samba esporte fino*, released in Brazil, was also released internationally by Mr. Bongo, but with the title *Carolina*.

42. *João-de-barro* is a South American bird that builds its house out of clay.

2. Radio Transvestism and the Gendered Soundscape in Buenos Aires, 1930s–1940s

Initial research for this article was undertaken with support from the National Endowment for the Humanities and the University of Louisville. I am thankful to the many people who provided helpful suggestions and critiques on this project, including Pablo Ben, Gabriela Cano, Brad Fugate, Michele Hilmes, Matt Karush, Kate Lacey, Andrea Matallana, Kristen McLeary, Jamie Medhurst, Mary Roldán, David Suisman, and the editors and anonymous reviewers of this edited volume.

1. "Mas que ridículo," *Antena* 34 (January 9, 1932), 3.

2. Marjorie Garber, *Vested Interests: Cross Dressing and Cultural Anxiety* (New York: HarperCollins, 1992), 32.

3. See Carlos Octavio Bunge, *Los envenenados: escenas de la vida argentina del siglo XIX* (Madrid: Escasa-Calpe, 1926); cited in Osvaldo Bazán, *Historia de la homosexualidad en la Argentina: de la conquista de América al siglo XXI* (Buenos Aires: Marea, 2004).

4. Ben Sifuentes-Járegui, *Transvestism, Masculinity and Latin American Literature: Genders Share Flesh* (New York: Palgrave MacMillan, 2002), 2.

5. John Strausbaugh describes the radio performances of Amos 'n' Andy as "aural blackface." John Strausbaugh, *Black Like You, Blackface, Whiteface, Insult and Imitation in American Popular Culture* (New York: Tarcher, 2007),

225. See also Susan J. Douglas's discussion of "linguistic slapstick" and the "racial ventriloquism" of Amos 'n' Andy in *Listening In: Radio and the American Imagination* (Minneapolis: University of Minnesota Press, 2004), 104–10.

6. Matthew Murray, "'The Tendency to Deprave and Corrupt Morals': Regulation and Irregular Sexuality in Golden Age Radio Comedy," in *Radio Reader: Essays in the Cultural History of Radio*, ed. Michele Hilmes and Jason Loviglio (London & New York: Routledge, 2002), 135–56.

7. Emily Thompson, *The Soundscape of Modernity: Architectural Acoustics and the Culture of Listening in America, 1900–1933* (Cambridge, MA: MIT Press, 2004), 1.

8. Helmi Järviluoma, Pirkko Moisala, and Anni Vilkko, *Gender and Qualitative Methods* (London: Sage, 2003), 85.

9. See R. Murray Schafer, *Soundscape: Our Sonic Environment and the Tuning of the World* (Destiny Books, 1993); Mark M. Smith, *Listening to Nineteenth-Century America* (Chapel Hill: University of North Carolina Press, 2001), 28–30; Kathleen Hall Jamieson, *Eloquence in an Electronic Age: The Transformation of Political Speechmaking* (New York: Oxford University Press, 1988), 67–79.

10. The concept of the "disembodied" female voice is most associated with Kaja Silverman's *The Acoustic Mirror: The Female Voice in Psychoanalysis and Cinema* (Bloomington: Indiana University Press, 1988). The concept is applied to radio in Michele Hilmes, *Radio Voices: American Broadcasting, 1922–1952* (Minneapolis: University of Minnesota Press), 130–50.

11. Anne Karpf, *The Human Voice: How This Extraordinary Instrument Reveals Essential Clues About Who We Are* (New York: Bloomsbury, 2006), 153–95.

12. Michel Chion, *The Voice in Cinema*, trans. Claudia Gorbman (New York: Columbia University Press, 1999), 17–29. See also Mladen Dolar, *A Voice and Nothing More* (Cambridge, MA: MIT Press, 2006), 60–71.

13. There is a lot of literature on the subject of female voice and film sound. The best, in my opinion, is Britta Sjogren, *Into the Vortex: Female Voice and Paradox in Film* (Champaign: University of Illinois Press, 2005).

14. Edward D. Miller, *Emergency Broadcasting and 1930s American Radio* (Philadelphia: Temple University Press, 2003), 6.

15. Jorge Salessi, "The Argentine Dissemination of Homosexuality, 1890–1914," *Journal of the History of Sexuality* 4, no. 3 (January 1994): 337–68.

16. See, for example, Lenard R. Berlanstein, "Breeches and Breaches: Cross-Dress Theater and the Culture of Gender Ambiguity in Modern France," *Comparative Studies in Society and History* 38, no. 2 (1996): 338–69, and Ursula K.

Heise, "Transvestism and the Stage Controversy in Spain and England, 1580–1680," *Theater Journal* 44, no. 3 (1992): 357–74. For an interesting discussion of gender and other masquerades during Argentine Carnival, see Micol Seigel, "Cocoliche's Romp: Fun with Nationalism at Argentina's Carnival," *The Drama Review* 44, no. 2 (2000): 56–83.

17. Radio magazines and other publications often provided listeners with a visual image to go along with the voice they were hearing, but that reference was never universal or immediate. This was particularly true in radio's early days, when radio publications contained far fewer photographs.

18. "Mas que ridículo," *Antena* 34 (January 9, 1932): 3.

19. "Ridículo y hasta inmoral," *Antena* 35 (January 16, 1932): 3.

20. "Mas que ridículo," *Antena* 34 (January 9, 1932): 3.

21. "Ridículo y hasta inmoral," *Antena* 35 (January 16, 1932): 3.

22. Ibid.

23. Sylvia Molloy, "Memories of Tango," *ReVista* 7, no. 1 (Fall 2007), 9. See also Sirena Pellarolo, "Queering Tango: Glitches in the Hetero-National Matrix of a Liminal Cultural Production," *Theater Journal* 60, no. 3 (2008): 409–31.

24. Anahí Viladrich, "Neither Virgins nor Whores: Tango Lyrics and Gender Representations in the Tango World," *Journal of Popular Culture* 39, no. 2 (2006): 272–93. See also Matt Karush's discussion of Maizani in *Culture of Class: Radio and Cinema in the Making of a Divided Argentina, 1920–1945.* (Durham, NC: Duke University Press, forthcoming).

25. "Reacción esperada," *Antena* 38 (6 February 1932): 3.

26. See Hilmes, *Radio Voices*, 141–44; Donna Halper, *Invisible Stars: A Social History of Women and Broadcasting* (New York: M.E. Sharpe, 2001), 39–47; Katherine Lacey, *Feminine Frequencies: Gender, German Radio, and the Public Sphere, 1923–1945* (Ann Arbor: University of Michigan Press, 1996), 193–220.

27. See also Salessi's discussion of anarchist female activist orators and their association with "feminine uranism" in "The Argentine Dissemination of Homosexuality," 345–46.

28. See Christine Ehrick, "'Savage Dissonance': Gender, Voice, and Women's Radio Speech in Argentina, 1930–1945," in *Sound in the Age of Mechanical Reproduction*, eds. David Suisman and Susan Strasser (Philadelphia: University of Pennsylvania Press, 2009), 69–93.

29. Bazán, *Historia de la homosexualidad,* 215–17.

30. For more on the ideology of the Argentine Right in this era, see Federico Finchelstein, *Transatlantic Fascism: Ideology, Violence and the Sacred in Argentina and Italy, 1919–1945* (Durham, NC: Duke University Press, 2010).

See also Sandra McGee Deutch, *Las Derechas: The Extreme Right in Argentina, Brazil, and Chile, 1890–1939* (Stanford, CA: Stanford University Press, 1999).

31. Andrea Matallana, *'Locos por la radio': Una historia social de la radiofonía en la Argentina, 1923–1947* (Buenos Aires: Prometeo Libros, 2006), 144.

32. Ibid., 145.

33. Lawrence La Fountain-Stokes, "Trans/bolero/drag/migration: Music, Cultural Translation and Disaporic Puerto Rican Theatricalities," *Women's Studies Quarterly* 36, no. 3–4 (2008): 191.

34. Ulanovsky, *Días de radio,* 129.

35. "Será Cierto?" *Radiolandia*, June 27, 1942.

36. "Elvira Ríos – es un hombre?" *Cine Radio Actualidad,* July 2, 1943.

37. *Cine Radio Actualidad,* July 9, 1943.

38. "Elvira Ríos ha sufrido un lamentable accidente," *Radiolandia*, March 18, 1944.

39. "Elvira Ríos sigue en danza: Ahora la fantasía popular la cree un espia," *Radiolandia*, September 4, 1943.

40. "Elvira Ríos: Ni espía, ni toxicomana, ni rusa, ni lo otro," *Antena*, September 2, 1943.

41. In August 1943, shortly after the Ríos rumors began, Spanish singer Miguel de Molina—labeled in Spain as a *rojo maricón*—was expelled from Argentina because of his sexual identity. He returned in 1946 by invitation from First Lady Eva Perón. See Bazán, *Historia de la homosexualidad,* 229–37.

42. Donna J. Guy, *Sex and Danger in Buenos Aires: Prostitution, Family and Nation in Argentina* (Lincoln: University of Nebraska Press, 1991), 180–91. See also Bazán, *Historia de la homosexualidad,* 274–77.

43. Ulanovsky, *Días de radio,* 139.

44. Murray, "The Tendency to Deprave and Corrupt Morals," 146–47.

45. Pedro De Paoli, *Función social de la radiotelefonía* (Buenos Aires: Editorial "El Ateneo," 1943), 161.

46. Although direct evidence is lacking, one must also consider the possibility that the regime's homophobia and anti-Semitism were converging here. Marjorie Garber reminds us that European anti-Semitism has a long history of depicting Jewish men as both "degenerate" and "effeminate" and that much of that was presented via "the way [male] Jews supposedly spoke." See Garber, *Vested Interests,* 226.

47. De Paoli, *Función social de la radiotelefonía,* 148. For more on the structures of Argentine melodrama, see Matthew B. Karush, "Populism, Melodrama, and the Market: The Mass Cultural Origins of Peronism," in *The New Cultural History of Peronism: Power and Identity in Mid-Twentieth-Century*

Argentina, eds. Matthew B. Karush and Oscar Chamosa (Durham, NC: Duke University Press, 2010), 21–51.

48. See, for example, Mariano Ben Plotkin, *Mañana es San Perón: A Cultural History of Perón's Argentina*, trans. Keith Zahniser (Wilmington, DE: Scholarly Resources, 2003).

49. Pablo Sirvén, *Perón y los medios de comunicación, 1943–1955* (Buenos Aires: Centro Editor de América Latina, 1984), 56. See also Ulanovsky, *Días de radio*, 153–54.

50. República Argentina, Ministerio del Interior, *Manual de instrucciones para las estaciones de radiodifusión* (Buenos Aires: Servicio Oficial, 1947), 12; cited in Matallana, *Locos por la radio*, 49.

51. For more on sexuality and the pleasures of radio listening, see Allison McCracken, "'God's Gift to Us Girls': Crooning, Gender and the Re-Creation of American Popular Song, 1928–1933," *American Music* 17, no. 4 (1999): 365–95. For an in-depth discussion of the pleasures audiences derived from the "melodramatic overflow" of radio drama in Latin America, see Reynaldo González, *Llorar es un placer* (Havana: Editorial Letras Cubanas, 1988).

52. See Bryan McCann, *Hello, Hello Brazil: Popular Music in the Making of Modern Brazil* (Durham, NC: Duke University Press, 2004), 181–214.

53. Jacob Smith, *Vocal Tracks: Performance and Sound Media* (Berkeley: University of California Press, 2008), 177.

3. How to Do Things with Waves: United States Radio and Latin America in the Times of the Good Neighbor

Epigraph: Gordon W. Allport and Hadley Cantril, *The Psychology of Radio* (New York: Arno Press, 1971), 20.

1. Allport and Cantril, *The Psychology of Radio*, 20.

2. Benedict Anderson, *Imagined Communities* (London: Verso, 2003). Few historians have followed Anderson's suggestions on the role of "print capitalism" in the rise of early nationalism in the Americas. Nevertheless, *Imagined Communities* has been immensely influential in communication research and media studies dealing with later stages of the nation-building process. For a recent empirical effort to spell out how the mass media and, particularly, news broadcasts may shape a sense of belonging to a national community, see, for example, Paul Frosh and Gadi Wolfsfeld, "ImagiNation: News Discourse, Nationhood and Civil Society," *Media, Culture and Society* 29, no. 1 (2007): 105–29.

3. Paddy Scannell, "For-Anyone-As-Someone Structures," *Media, Culture*

and Society 22, no. 1 (2000): 5–24, 9, 12. For our limited purposes here, I will not discuss the conceptual differences in the approach proposed by Scannell and Anderson.

4. Quoted in Michele Hilmes and Jason Loviglio, eds., *Radio Reader: Essays in the Cultural History of Radio* (London: Routledge, 2002), xi.

5. David Morley and Kevin Robins, *Spaces of Identity: Global Media, Electronic Landscapes, and Cultural Boundaries* (London: Routledge, 1995), 66.

6. Jesús Martín-Barbero, "Communication from Culture: The Crisis of the National and the Emergence of the Popular," *Media, Culture and Society* 10, no. 4 (1988): 455–56.

7. Karl Deutsch, *Nationalism and Social Communication: An Inquiry into the Foundation of Nationality* (Cambridge, MA: John Wiley & Sons, 1953), 77.

8. On the emergence of "print capitalism" and further conditions that gave rise to the basic morphology of modern nationalism, see Anderson, *Imagined Communities*, chapter 3.

9. Allport and Cantril, *Psychology of Radio*, 21. For a more recent analysis of ubiquitous and continual "flagging" that reminds audiences on a daily basis of their national place in a world of nations, see Michael Billig, *Banal Nationalism* (London: Sage, 1995).

10. Susan J. Douglas, *Listening In: Radio and the American Imagination* (New York: Random House, 1999), 218.

11. Thus the Empire Service's soon familiar signal, the chimes of Big Ben, was the product of an inquiry among listeners; see Emma Robertson, "'Get a Real Kick Out of Big Ben': BBC Versions of Britishness on the Empire and General Overseas Service, 1932–1948," *Historical Journal of Film, Radio and Television* 28, no. 4 (2008): 459–73.

12. Michele Hilmes, "Radio Nations: The Importance of Transnational Media Study," in *Atlantic Communications: The Media in American and German History from the Seventeenth to the Twentieth Century*, eds. Norbert Finzsch and Ursula Lehmkuhl (Oxford: Berg Publishers, 2004), 299–308.

13. Quoted in David Morley, *Home Territories: Media, Mobility and Identity* (London, New York: Routledge, 2000), 106.

14. For a critique of Scannell's "we-ness," see, for instance, Morley, *Home Territories*, 108–20.

15. Derek W. Vaillant, "Sounds of Whiteness: Local Radio, Racial Formation, and Public Culture in Chicago, 1921–1935," *American Quarterly* 54, no. 1 (2002): 26; see also Alexander Russo, "A Darken(ed) Figure on the Airwaves. Race, Nation and the *Green Hornet*," in Hilmes and Loviglio, *Radio Reader*, 257–76.

16. Michele Hilmes, *Radio Voices: American Broadcasting, 1922–1952* (Minneapolis: University of Minnesota Press, 1997), 230–70.

17. The inclusion of such programs into mainstream broadcasting was accompanied by considerable frictions; for details, see Barbara Dianne Savage, *Broadcasting Freedom: Radio, War, and the Politics of Race, 1938–1948* (Chapel Hill: University of North Carolina Press, 1999); Judith E. Smith, *Visions of Belonging: Family Stories, Popular Culture, and Postwar Democracy, 1940–1960* (New York: Columbia University Press, 2004), 36–37; Diane Selig, *Americans All: The Cultural Gifts Movement* (Cambridge, MA: Harvard University Press, 2008), 237–67.

18. Lyman Bryson and Dorothy Rowden, "Radio as an Agency for National Unity," *The Annals of the American Academy* 244 (1946): 142–43.

19. African American activists continued to be frustrated by radio, but never before had racial issues been probed so openly on U.S. networks as during World War II. For details and further references, see Hilmes, *Radio Voices*, 258, 263.

20. See, for example, the fate of the so-called Pan-American frequencies that had been set aside for inter-American programming but had been left idle until the late 1930s. Gisela Cramer, "The Rockefeller Foundation and Pan American Radio," in *Patronizing the Public: American Philanthropic Support for Communication, Culture, and the Humanities in the Twentieth Century*, ed. William Buxton, 77–99 (Lanham, MD: Lexington Books, 2009).

21. This does not hold true for some areas in the U.S. Southwest and for transnational broadcasting along the United States–Mexico border. Unfortunately, for reasons of space, I cannot expand on such exceptions. On the tango and rumba "rages" of the 1920s and 1930s, see John Storm Roberts, *The Latin Tinge: The Impact of Latin American Music on the United States* (New York: Oxford University Press, 1999).

22. The reasons why broadcasting in general is more susceptible than print media to government pressures are explained in Paul Starr, *The Creation of the Media: Political Origins of Modern Communications* (New York: Basic-Books, 2004), 363–70. In the late 1930s, broadcasters had additional reasons for complying with government suggestions, since they feared increased intervention and, particularly, the establishment of a government-controlled station to broadcast to Latin America. For a brief summary and further references, see Cramer, "The Rockefeller Foundation and Pan American Radio."

23. "Brave New World," *Time*, Nov. 15, 1937. These and following quotes from *Time* magazine were retrieved from the Time Magazine Online Archive at http://www.time.com/time/archive.

24. Philip Leonard Green, *Pan American Progress* (New York: Hastings House, 1942), 86–87.

25. For a brief introduction on the OIAA, see Gisela Cramer and Ursula Prutsch, "Nelson A. Rockefeller's Office of Inter-American Affairs and Record Group 229," *The Hispanic American Historical Review* 86, no.4 (2006): 785–806.

26. Latin America was widely perceived as constituting the "soft underbelly" of the United States. For a detailed analysis of the rise, pervasiveness, and particularities of U.S. threat perceptions, see Uwe Lübken, *Bedrohliche Nähe. Die USA und die nationalsozialistische Herausforderung in Lateinamerika, 1937–1945* (Stuttgart: Steiner, 2004).

27. Hubert Herring, *Good Neighbors: Argentina, Brazil, Chile and Seventeen Other Countries* (New Haven, CT: Yale University Press, 1941), 327.

28. Brazil, for example, was very often and positively reported upon. This reflected not only the relative importance of Brazil as a war ally but also the fact that the Vargas government came to sponsor news and commentary programs in the United States. For further details, see Antonio Pedro Tota, *O imperialismo sedutor: A americanização do Brasil na época da Segunda Guerra* (São Paulo: Companhia Das Letras, 2005).

29. Thus, to give but one example, Jack Starr Hunt reported on a regular basis from Mexico for Mutal Broadcasting System (MBS). See Belmont Farley, "Radio and Pan American Relations," *The Phi Delta Kappan* 24, no. 3 (1941): 109.

30. Rockefeller's OIAA not only exerted pressure on the news agencies to start a Latin American news roundup as a specialized service, but it also prepared scripts on how to introduce and close the *News of the Other Americas*. See letter from Don Francisco to Station Managers, June 29, 1942, National Archives at College Park (hereafter NARA II), Record Group (hereafter RG) 229, Entry (hereafter E) 1, General Records (hereafter GR), Central Files (hereafter CF), Box 256, File: News Broadcasts to June 1942.

31. John Dunning, *On the Air: The Encyclopedia of Old-Time Radio* (New York: Oxford University Press, 1998), 49.

32. "Radio: Muchacho Meets Muchacha," *Time*, March 16, 1942.

33. Don Francisco to Sylvester L. Weaver, Feb. 23, 1942, and Ross Worthington to Don Francisco, Feb. 23, 1942 (NARA II, RG 229, E 1, GR, CF, Box 244, 3. Information. Radio) File: Down Mexico Way.

34. For further details on *Pan American Holiday,* see the *New York Times,* May 31, 1942, X10; *Washington Post,* Aug. 30, 1942, L9.

35. In academic circles, Herbert E. Bolton's approach did not make too

much headway, but by the early 1940s, many agencies promoting inter-American understanding viewed Bolton as one of their leading experts in the field. Some of his students, moreover, joined the Latin American desk of the Department of State and other government agencies. On the rise and decline of the Western Hemisphere idea, see Russell M. Magnaghi, *Herbert E. Bolton and the Historiography of the Americas* (Westport, CT: Greenwood Press, 1998); Arthur P. Whitaker, *The Western Hemisphere Idea: Its Rise and Decline* (Ithaca, NY: Cornell University Press, 1954); Lewis Hanke, ed., *Do Americans Have a Common History? A Criticism of the Bolton Theory* (New York: Knopf, 1964).

36. Farley, "Radio and Pan American Relations," 108. (Farley was the director of public relations and radio coordinator of the National Education Association.)

37. According to the *New York Times* (Feb. 23, 1941, X12, and Aug. 10, 1941, X10), more than one thousand delegates were expected to attend each of the two conferences. The second conference took place at the Mexican National Palace of Fine Arts, under the auspices of the Mexican government.

38. By late 1940, *Cadena de las Americas* on CBS had affiliated sixty-four stations in eighteen Latin American countries, obliging each of them to carry at least one hour of CBS-prepared broadcasts every day. However, I have seen no evidence suggesting that the educational programs prepared by the *School of the Air of the Americas* were very successful as an item for rebroadcasts in Latin America.

39. Gilbert Chase, "Music of the New World," *Music Educators Journal* 30, no. 2 (1943): 17–18, 49. This cycle was conceived by musicologist Carleton Sprague Smith.

40. "Radio: Voice of History," *Time*, April 3, 1944.

41. These scripts are located at NARA II, RG 229, E 1, GR, CF, Box 244, 3. Information. Radio. Local Committee and Project Authorization Programs, File: Inter-American University of the Air.

42. Report of the Activities of the Radio Division. Coordinator of inter-American Affairs, May 20, 1942 (NARA II, RG 229, E 81. Records of the Radio Division. Miscellaneous Reports and Issuances, Box 964, File: Report of Radio Division to State Department).

43. This is a clear contrast to earlier depictions of Latin American heroes as analyzed by Fredrick B. Pike, *The United States and Latin America: Myths and Stereotypes of Civilization and Nature* (Austin: University of Texas Press, 1992), 61–70.

44. These observations are based on a variety of *Salute* scripts found scattered throughout the archival holdings of RG 229 (NARA II).

45. See, for instance, Ricardo D. Salvatore, "North American Travel Narratives and the Ordering/Othering of South America (c.1810–1860)," *Journal of Historical Sociology* 9, no.1 (1996): 85–110.

46. For example, mention was made that some of the Latin American universities were older than Harvard.

47. Don Francisco to Station Managers, April 4, 1942, annexed script, p. 3 (NARA II, RG 229, E 1, GR, CF, Box 331, 3. Information. Radio. Country files. Cuba. Folder: Scripts and Material).

48. One country, however, received a somewhat different treatment after 1941: Argentina. For reasons of space, I cannot discuss this particular case here.

49. Don Francisco to Station Managers, April 4, 1942, annexed script, p. 1–2 (NARA II, RG 229, E 1, GR, CF, Box 331, 3. Information. Radio. Country files. Cuba. Folder: Scripts and Material).

50. Francisco to Station Managers, Aug. 24, 1942, annexed script, p. 2, 4 (NARA II, RG 229, E 1, GR, CF, Box 331, 3. Information. Radio. Country files. Cuba. Folder: Scripts and Material).

51. *Hello Americans* program on *Bolívar's Idea,* Jan. 31, 1943, p. 6 (NARA II, RG 229, E 1, GR, CF, Box 255, 3. Information. Radio. Programs, Dramatic. File: B-RA-1515 scripts Orson Welles).

52. "Radio: Orson at War," *Time*, Nov. 30, 1942. Indeed, I have seen no trace of tensions comparable to the conflict with RKO in the OIAA's archival holdings.

53. Robert Stam, "Tropical Multiculturalism," in *A Comparative History of Race in Brazilian Cinema and Culture* (Durham, NC: Duke University Press, 1997), 111.

54. "Other foreign colonies bit their nails in vexation at not having thought of the project and the good-will earned certainly was worth the time involved" reported the OIAA's Brazilian Division on the success of the birthday gala. See Report of the Brazilian Division, May 25, 1942, p. 2 (RAC, NAR Personal Washington Files, RG 4 CIAA, Box 4, Folder 30: Coordinator of Inter-American Affairs of the United States of America); see also Tota, *O imperialismo sedutor*, 120–26; Ursula Prutsch, *Creating Good Neighbors? Die Kultur- und Wirtschaftspolitik der USA in Lateinamerika, 1940–1946* (Stuttgart: Steiner, 2008), 241–42.

55. Some of the programs from this series are still available on the Internet, at http://www.archive.org/details/Adventures_of_the_Seahound. The series survived into the postwar period but with contents unrelated to Latin America.

56. This series survived for only a few months as a government-sponsored

project. By the middle of 1942, the OIAA discontinued its support, despite rather favorable audience ratings. The OIAA's reasons are not entirely clear, but it probably feared congressional critique. To spend taxpayer's money during a war on a lighthearted and at times rather silly show was somewhat of an institutional risk for the agency. For further information, see NARA II, RG 229, E 1, GR, CF, Box 245, 3. Information. Radio. Programs, File: Ripley, Robt. Believe it or not.

57. On the sheer quantity of such insertions into commercially sponsored programs, see Report of the Activities of the Radio Division. Coordinator of inter-American Affairs, May 20, 1942, p. 2 (NARA II, RG 229, E 81. Records of the Radio Division. Misc. Reports and Issuances, Box 964).

58. These included, for example, M. H. Aylesworth, former president of NBC; Sylvester "Pat" Weaver, later to become president of NBC; James W. Young and Don Francisco, top executives of the J. Walter Thompson advertising agency; Karl A. Bickel, former president of United Press and chairman of Scripps-Howard Radio.

59. One of the *Cavalcade of America* shows was Orson Welles's *Columbus Day 1942*. A reprint can be found in Erik Barnouw, *Radio Drama in Action: Twenty-Five Plays of a Changing World* (New York: Rinehart, 1945), 1–16.

60. Weekly Report of the Communications Division's Activities, Dec. 18, 1941 (33rd report), p. 2, and following reports (NARA II, RG 229, E 1, GR, CF, 4. Administration. Reports. Weekly. Box 446. Folder: Communications Reports).

61. The list included, to name the more prominent examples broadcast by the larger networks: *The Breakfast Club, Club Matinee, The Family Hour, The Army Hour, Hobby Lobby, George Burns and Gracie Allen, Fibber McGee and Molly, Johnny Presents, Prescott Presents, Bob Hope Variety Program, Take It or Leave It, Xavier Cugat, NBC Symphony Orchestra, Fred Waring, Gabriel Heatter,* and the *March of Time* (NARA II, RG 229, E 87. Records of the Department of Information. Education Division. Project Files, NDCar-58 to NDCar-78, Box 1163; Folder: Pan American Day Exhibits, Correspondence, Misc. and Fiestas—P NDCar-71).

62. "Mouths South," *Time,* June 1, 1941.

63. For program examples, see Farley, "Radio and Pan-American Relations," 109.

64. "Mouths South," *Time,* June 1, 1941.

65. Ibid.

66. The information on *Viva America* was culled from daily radio schedules as published by the *New York Times* and the *Washington Post,* 1942–1948.

67. The show was advertised as "a kaleidoscopic picture of the Western Hemisphere in music, story, and song," with guest stars each week. Hilmes, *Radio Voices*, 234.

68. Farley, "Radio and Pan American Relations," 109.

69. On *The Americas Speak,* see Farley, "Radio and Pan American Relations," 109.

70. For an example of ubiquitous "flagging," see the description of a Pan-American musical event broadcast over the CBS domestic and Latin American partner networks in "Music Fiesta Held at Carnegie Hall," *New York Times*, Oct. 29, 1941, 27.

71. "Music: Formidable," *Time*, Sep. 27, 1948.

72. Tota, *O imperialismo sedutor*, 101 (the translation is mine).

73. This is how the episode "Trapped Below" ends. The show is accessible at http://www.archive.org/details/Adventures_of_the_Seahound.

74. Quoted in Tota, *O imperialismo sedutor*, 137.

75. Ibid., 101 (the translation is mine).

76. I do not wish to suggest that such visions were wholly absent in the educational and informational content discussed here, but it seems to me that they are more prominent in the entertainment genres.

77. Quoted in Andrew Crisell, *Understanding Radio* (London: Routledge, 1994), 190.

78. See, for instance, the space given to the Good Neighbor programs in the following radio review: Kenneth G. Bartlett, "Radio War Programs," *Quarterly Journal of Speech* 29, no. 1 (1943): 100–103.

79. Clippings from *Variety*, found in RG 229, E 1, GR, CF, Box 255, 3. Information. Radio. Programs, Dramatic. File: B-RA-1515.

80. Some 200,000 of such maps were sent out; for further details, see Adventures of the Sea Hound (NARA II, RG 229, E 1, GR, CF, Box 250, 3. Information. Radio. Programs); Report Drafts 1944, Phase III, p. 50 (RAC, RG 4, Box 11, Folder 84).

81. Quoted in Tota, *O imperialismo sedutor*, 117.

82. Ibid., 206.

83. On this and other shows for Pan American Day 1942, see NARA II, RG 229, E 87. Records of the Department of Information. Education Division. Project Files, NDCar-58 to NDCar-78, Box 1163; Folder: Pan American Day Exhibits, Correspondence, Misc and Fiestas–P NDCar-71.

84. CBS News, April 16, 1943 (NARA II, RG 229, E 1, GR, CF, Box 245, 3. Information. Radio. Programs, File: Andre Kostelanetz).

85. See Farley, "Radio and Pan American Relations," 109. The background

for CBS, NBC, and other networks seeking affiliations in Latin America is explained in Fred Fejes, *Imperialism, Media and the Good Neighbor: New Deal Foreign Policy and United States Shortwave Broadcasting to Latin America* (Norwood, NJ: Ablex, 1986), 127–31.

86. *New York Times*, Feb. 23, 1941, X10; Dunning, *On the Air*, 706. On the *Vox Pop* success story, see also Jason Loviglio, "Vox Pop: Network Radio and the Voice of the People," in Hilmes and Loviglio, *Radio Reader*, 89–111.

87. In 1930s Sweden, for instance, even seemingly innocuous programs such as the weather forecasts served such ends. As Orvar Löfgren observes, "In the daily shipping forecast, the names of the coastal observation posts of Sweden were read like a magic chant, as outposts encircling the nation" (Quoted in Morley, *Home Territories*, 116).

88. Katherine Graham, "Need for Hemisphere Unity Gives Pan American Day New Meaning," *Washington Post*, March 13, 1941, B9.

89. For a musicologist's verdict, see Thomas George Caracas García, "American Views of Brazilian Musical Culture: Villa-Lobos's *Magdalena* and Brazilian Popular Music," *Journal of Popular Culture* 37, no. 4 (2004): 634–64.

90. For a brief overview, see Virginia Prewett, *The Americas and Tomorrow* (Philadelphia: Blakiston, 1944), 278–81.

91. For some, the Latin American hype at the expense of Cervantes and other classical writers was going too far. See Christopher S. Espinosa, "An Open Letter to Mr. Nelson Rockefeller, Coordinator of Inter-American Affairs," *Hispania* 27, no. 3 (1944): 344–45.

92. Donald M. Dozer, *Are We Good Neighbors? Three Decades of Inter-American Relations, 1930–1960* (Gainesville: University of Florida Press, 1959), 387–88.

93. Quoted in Hilmes, *Radio Voices*, 263.

94. Ibid.

95. This is a suggestion informed by recent theoretical and empirical works by constructivists in International Relations. See, for instance, David L. Rousseau, *Identifying Threats and Threatening Identities: The Social Construction of Realism and Liberalism* (Palo Alto, CA: Stanford University Press, 2006).

96. Memorandum A. L. Chapman, An Evaluation of the "Know Your Neighbor Radio Programs." Bureau of Research and Education by Radio, University of Texas (NARA II, RG 229, E 1, GR, CF, 3. Information. Science and Education. Education. Schools and Institutions, Box 386, Folder: B-SE-1619 NDCar-10). See also Arthur L. Brandon, "Know Your Neighbor," *Phi Delta Kappan* 24, no. 3 (1941): 110–12.

97. The overall results were published in Hadley Cantril, *Public Opinion 1935–1946* (Princeton, NJ: Princeton University Press, 1951), 502.

4. Weapons of the Geek: Romantic Narratives, Sonic Technologies, and Tinkerers in 1930s Santiago, Cuba

Research for this chapter was funded by a Social Sciences and Humanities Research Council Individual Research Grant. I gratefully acknowledge the people who contributed to or commented on earlier drafts, including Alexander Dawson, Courtney Booker, Christine Ehrick, Andrew Grant Wood, and the two anonymous reviewers of this volume.

1. *La Independencia,* January 10, 1923, 4. On technology, space and time, see among others Michael Taussig, *Mimesis and Alterity: A Particular History of the Senses* (New York: Routledge Press, 1993); Stephen Kern, *The Culture of Time and Space, 1880–1918* (Cambridge, MA: Harvard University Press, 2003).

2. Richard Rath, "Hearing American History," *Journal of American History* 95, no. 2 (2008): 430–31; Lisa Gitelman and Geoffrey B. Pingree, eds., *New Media: 1740–1915* (Cambridge, MA: MIT Press, 2003); *La Independencia,* January 10, 1923.

3. Friedrich Kittler, *Gramophone, Film, Typewriter,* trans. Geoffrey Winthrop-Young and Michael Wutz (Palo Alto: Stanford University Press, 1999).

4. Archivo Historico Provincial de Santiago (hereafter, AHPS), Fondo Audiencia de Oriente, Tribunal de Urgencia, Juicios Establecidos Por Huelgas, 13 Agosto al 10 Septiembre, 1934. "Expediente que trata de la causa contra Angel Aguilera Baez, por penetrar en la oficina de correos y extraer tres clavijas de contacto, con el fin de impeder que los empleados trabajaran con motivo de la huelga de comunicaciones," 2.

5. Richard Coyne, *Technoromanticism: Digital Narrative, Holism and the Romance of the Real* (Cambridge, MA: MIT Press, 2001), 19.

6. David Scott, *Conscripts of Modernity: The Tragedy of Colonial Enlightenment* (Durham, NC: Duke University Press, 2004).

7. Scott compares two editions of C. L. R. James's book *The Black Jacobins: Toussaint L'Ouverture and the San Domingo Revolution* (London: Secker and Warburg, 1938) and *The Black Jacobins: Toussaint L'Ouverture and the San Domingo Revolution,* 2nd ed. rev. (New York: Vintage, 1963).

8. Stuart Hall, Interview with David Scott, *BOMB* 90 (Winter 2005), http://www.bombsite.com/issues/90/articles/2711.

9. Charles Tilly, *Contentious Performances* (New York: Cambridge University Press, 2008).

10. Dwayne R. Winseck and Robert M. Pike, *Communication and Empire: Media, Markets and Globalization, 1860–1930* (Durham, NC: Duke University Press, 2007).

11. Pedro Pruna, *Historia de la ciencia y la tecnología en Cuba* (Havana: Editorial Científico Técnica, 2006).

12. Oscar Luis López, *La radio en Cuba* (Havana: Editorial Letras Cubanas, 1998); Reynaldo González, *Llorar es un placer* (Havana: Editorial Letras Cubanas, 2002).

13. Yuzo Takahshi, "A Network of Tinkerers: The Advent of the Radio and Television Receiver Industry in Japan," *Technology and Culture* 41 (July 2000): 460–84.

14. Kristen Haring, *Ham Radio's Technical Culture* (Cambridge, MA: MIT Press, 2007).

15. Juan Maria Ravelo, *Páginas de ayer: Narraciones de Santiago de Cuba* (Manzanillo: Editorial El Arte, 1943).

16. Louis A. Pérez Jr., *Cuba under the Platt Amendment, 1902–1934* (Pittsburgh, PA: University of Pittsburgh Press, 1986); Robert Whitney, *State Revolution in Cuba: Mass Mobilization and Political Change* (Chapel Hill: University of North Carolina Press, 2001).

17. Ravelo, *Paginas de ayer*, 165–66.

18. Ibid., 171.

19. Stuart Hall Interview with David Scott, *BOMB*.

20. Ibid.

21. "Two Wounded in Cuba" *New York Times* (hereafter, *NYT*), March 3, 1934, 3; "Mendieta Orders New Curb on Cuba," *NYT*, March 7, 1934, 4.

22. J. D. Phillips, "Vast Cuban Strike Defies Decree Ban," *NYT*, March 9, 1934, 1.

23. "Strike Emergency Declared in Cuba," *NYT*, March 8, 1934, 6.

24. "Cuban Declares Ban on Striking Unions," *NYT*, March 10, 1934, 1.

25. "Strikers Return to Work in Cuba," *NYT*, March 14, 1934, 20.

26. AHPS, Fondo Audiencia de Oriente, Tribunal de Defensa Nacional; Juicios establecidos por sabotajes y terrorismos. "Expediente instruido contra José Maria Blanco, por cometer un delito contra la estabilidad de la república consistiente en un sabotaje a los alambres que dan al centro telefónico—interrumpiendo completamente el servicio." 23 marzo al 23 abril, 1934.

27. J. D. Phillips, "New Strike Ties Up All Phones in Cuba," *NYT*, July 25, 1934, 4.

28. J. D. Phillips, "Cuba Takes Over Phone Company, American Owned, in Labor Row," *NYT*, August 9, 1934, 1.

29. "New Walkout Begun in Cuba," *NYT*, August 13, 1934, 7.

30. AHPS, Fondo Audiencia de Oriente. Tribunal de Urgencia. "Juicios Establecidos Por Huelgas. 13 Agosto al 13 Septiembre, 1934. "Expediente relacionado con la detención de José Antonio Pascual por acatar como bueno el movimiento de huelga de empleados de comunicaciones."

31. AHPS, Fondo Audiencia de Oriente. Tribunal de Urgencia. "Juicios Establecidos Por Huelgas. 13 Agosto al 13 Septiembre, 1934. "Expediente relacionado con la detención de José Antonio Pascual por acatar como bueno el movimiento de huelga de empleados de comunicaciones."

32. AHPS. Fondo Audiencia de Oriente, Tribunal de Urgencia. Juicios Establecidos Por Huelgas. 13 Agosto al 10 Septiembre, 1934. "Expediente que trata de la causa contra Angel Aguilera Baez, por penetrar en la oficina de correos y extraer tres clavijas de contacto, con el fin de impedir que los empleados trabajaran con motivo de la huelga de comunicaciones."

33. AHPS. Fondo Audiencia de Oriente, Tribunal de Urgencia. Juicios Establecidos Por Huelgas. 13 Agosto al 10 Septiembre, 1934. "Expediente que trata de la causa contra Angel Aguilera Baez, por penetrar en la oficina de correos y extraer tres clavijas de contacto, con el fin de impedir que los empleados trabajaran con motivo de la huelga de comunicaciones."

34. AHPS, Fondo Audiencia de Santiago, Sala de Urgencia. Juicios establecidos contra la estabilidad de la república. "Expediente que trata de la causa que se instruyó contra Domingo Gordin, por tener una estación de radio pirata, para que determinados elementos totalitarios se comunicaran con naciones extranjeras como alemania y otros paises fascistas."

5. Music, Media Spectacle, and the Idea of Democracy: The Case of DJ Kermit's "Góber"

1. Lydia Cacho, *Los demonios del Edén: El poder que protege a la pornografía infantil* (Mexico City: Grijalbo, 2005).

2. Nevertheless, the history of collaboration between Mexican media and the country's government shows a more complex hegemonic arrangement than the simple censorship/freedom-of-speech dichotomy suggested by this discourse. For a study on the relationship between the Mexican government and Televisa, the dominant private television network in Mexico before the 1990s, see Claudia Fernández and Andrew Paxman, *El tigre Emilio Azcárraga y su imperio de Televisa* (Mexico City: Grijalbo, 2000).

3. DJ Kermit's "Gober (Precioso)" was not the only EDM track inspired by the affair. DJ Christian composed "Precioso Mix," a track also based on samples from the telephone conversation. However, DJ Kermit's was the first and only

one to become a commercial success due to, among other things, its early media exposure. DJ Christian's "Precioso Mix" can be found at the following link: http://almaroja.blogspot.com/2006/04/precioso-mixuna-rola-la-preciosa .html.

4. Luis Felipe Castañeda, "Tiene el Góber su tema bailable," *Reforma,* February 14, 2006.

5. Lydia Cacho, *Memorias de una infamia* (Mexico City: Grijalbo, 2007), 168.

6. Ibid.

7. Since EDM is a music genre for the dance floor that rarely emphasizes lyrics, many practitioners of traditionally combative genres such as rock or hip hop tend to disregard it as nonpolitical music meant for bodily pleasure—not intellectual reflection. These misconceptions have also transferred to hip hop genres such as reggaeton, which emphasize the moving body. See Geoff Baker, "The Politics of Dancing: Reggaeton and Rap in Havana, Cuba" in *Reggaeton,* ed. Raquel Z. Rivera, Wayne Marshall, and Deborah Pacini Hernandez (Durham, NC: Duke University Press, 2009), 165–68.

8. Guy Debord, *Society of the Spectacle* (London: Rebel Press, 2006), 7–8.

9. Passed under pressure at the Mexican Congress by a majority of votes from the ruling party, PAN (Partido de Acción Nacional [National Action Party]), and the former ruling party, PRI (Partido Revolucionario Institucional [Institutional Revolutionary Party]), right before the 2006 presidential election, when both parties needed media exposure to overcome the lead of the leftist PRD (Partido de la Revolución Democrática [Democratic Revolution Party]), the law grants exclusive access to the country's digital frequency spectrum to the two largest television networks in the country: the privately owned Televisa and TV Azteca. Such a law consolidates the duopoly and its interests as the most powerful media network shaping public opinion in the country. Due to lobbying by and pressure from Televisa to pass it, the law came to be unofficially known as *Ley Televisa* (Televisa Law). See Andrea Becerra, "Quedó consumada en el Senado la ampliación del poder de radio y tv," *La Jornada,* March 31, 2006.

10. Out of their jurisdiction, the Puebla police had no legal power to arrest Cacho in Quintana Roo. This could have been done only by members of the Quintana Roo state police or by the federal police. Technically, the Puebla police kidnapped Cacho.

11. Cameron Scott, "Mexico's Most Wanted Journalist," *Mother Jones,* December 22, 2005, http://www.motherjones.com/interview/2007/05/cacho .html.

12. Francisco Reyes "DJ Kermit," personal interview, Mexico City, July 23, 2006.

13. Castañeda, "Tiene el Góber su tema bailable."

14. "Pega pirata 'mi góber precioso,'" *Reforma,* March 16, 2006.

15. Reyes, personal interview. Pasito duranguense is a substyle of banda music developed by Mexican Americans in Chicago. It is generally associated with a working-class sensibility as opposed to the urban cosmopolitanism of electronic music.

16. See Alejandro L. Madrid, *Nor-tec Rifa! Electronic Dance Music from Tijuana to the World* (New York: Oxford University Press, 2008), 90–91.

17. Theodor Adorno and Max Horkheimer, "The Culture Industry: Enlightenment as Mass Deception," in *The Cultural Studies Reader,* ed. Simon During (London: Routledge, 1993), 30–43.

18. Reyes, personal interview.

19. Minerva Ocampo Silva, "Antoine Clamaran & Matthew Dekay II," *Minerva o Atenea dilema es,* June 19, 2007, http://minervaoatenea.blogspot.com/2007/06/antoine-clamaran-matthew-dekay-ii.html. As I have already exposed, the conversation sampled in DJ Kermit's song is not between Marín and Succar Kuri, as Ocampo Silva states, but rather between Marín and Nacif.

20. Cacho, *Memorias de una infamia,* 122–29.

21. A rumor began to spread suggesting that the word *botella* (bottle) was code for "young girl" among pedophiles. Although the rumor was never fully confirmed, it became a central aspect in people's interpretations of the góber precioso affair. See Julián E. Puente Sánchez and David Casco Sosa, "Hendricks, Hamui y Martins: La triada intocable del Caribe," *Semanario Quehacer Político,* January 21, 2007; and "El cognac, botella bellísima," in *Awiwi,* http://awiwi.blogspot.com/2006/07/el-cognac-botella-bellsima_06.html. The cognac bottles are so important in the collective imaginary about the góber precioso affair that they are prominently featured on the cover of the commercial CD of DJ Kermit's track and remixes released by Musart.

22. Reyes, personal interview.

23. Ibid.

24. Katia D'Artígues, "Campos Elíseos: ¿Y ahora quién podrá defendernos?" *Vanguardia,* February 24, 2006.

25. "Da corte revés a Lydia Cacho; Marín libra juicio," *El Universal,* November 29, 2007.

26. Cacho, *Memorias de una infamia,* 199.

27. Ibid., 209–11.

6. Alba: Musical Temporality in the Carnival of Oruro, Bolivia

1. A. Beltrán Heredia, *El Carnaval de Oruro* (Oruro: Editorial Universitaria, 1956). This makes reference to Philippe III, the Spanish king who was the only surviving son of Philip II and Anne of Austria (the union of Spanish and Austrian monarchies). He reigned from 1598 until 1621, when he died. On the other hand, the name Oruro is a transliteration of "Uru Uru," making reference to the ancient inhabitants of the area (the Urus). Elsewhere, I develop some of the issues embedded in the sociopolitical and cultural dynamics of domination/denomination in Oruro—see Gonzalo Araoz, *Heavenly and Grotesque Imageries (Re)created in the Carnival of Oruro, Bolivia* (PhD diss., University of St Andrews, Scotland, 2003).

2. Herbert Klein, *Bolivia: The Evolution of a Multi-Ethnic Society* (New York: Oxford University Press, 1982).

3. Yves de la Menorval, personal interview, La Paz, March 8, 2002.

4. Araoz, *Heavenly and Grotesque Imageries (Re)created in the Carnival of Oruro, Bolivia.*

5. Ibid.

6. Carnival does not have a fixed date, as it is directly linked to Ash Wednesday and Easter Sunday, which fall on different dates each year. The first day of Carnival season varies with both national and local traditions. Local variations can be observed, for example, in European countries such as Germany, where Carnival begins on the feast of the Epiphany (January 6) in Bavaria but on November 11 at 11:11 am (eleventh month, day, hour, and minute) in Cologne and the Rhineland. In France, the celebration is restricted to Shrove Tuesday and *mi-carême,* or the Thursday of the third week of Lent. More generally, the commencement date is Quinquagesima Sunday (the Sunday before Ash Wednesday), and the termination is Shrove Tuesday, though, in some parts of Spain, Ash Wednesday is also included in Carnival celebrations—an observance that stems from a time when Ash Wednesday was not an integral part of Lent.

7. *Moqochinchis* are a soft drink made out of boiled dried peach.

8. Two of the most important musical and choreographic rhythms performed in the Carnival of Oruro. Although both are thoroughly discussed elsewhere (see Araoz, *Heavenly and Grotesque Imageries [Re]created in the Carnival of Oruro, Bolivia*), I will only make reference to the latter in this chapter.

9. Daniel Goldstein shows how Orureño residents of a migrant neighborhood in Cochabamba represent themselves through the development of a local fiesta modeled on the Oruro Carnival (Daniel Goldstein, "Performing Na-

tional Culture in a Bolivian Migrant Community," *Ethnology* 37, no. 2 [1998]: 117–32).

10. Obviously, there is also a spatial dimension that is directly linked to the temporal dimension, but I will concentrate here on the temporal sphere of events. For further details of the spatial sphere of the Alba Rite and the Oruro Carnival in general, see Araoz, *Heavenly and Grotesque Imageries (Re)created in the Carnival of Oruro, Bolivia.*

11. Richard Gale, ed., *The Philosophy of Time* (New York: Anchor Books, 1967), vii.

12. Araoz, *Heavenly and Grotesque Imageries (Re)created in the Carnival of Oruro, Bolivia,* vii. Bloch and Parry discuss the relation between the denial of the irreversible and terminal nature of death and the avoidance to recognize time's irreversibility in funerary rituals (Maurice Bloch and Johnathan Parry, ed., *Death and the Regeneration of Life* [Cambridge University Press, 1982]).

13. Edmund.R. Leach, *Replanteamiento de la Antropología* (Barcelona: Seix Barral, 1972), 207–8.

14. These "states" or "stages" clearly resemble those identified by Van Gennep in his analysis of rites of passage (Arnold Van Gennep, *The Rites of Passage* [Chicago: University of Chicago Press, 1960]).

15. Edmund.R. Leach, *Replanteamiento de la Antropología* (Barcelona: Seix Barral, 1972), 210.

16. Max Gluckmann, *Custom and Conflict in Africa* (Oxford: Blackwell, 1973).

17. Victor Turner, *The Ritual Process: Structure and Anti-Structure* (London: Routledge, 1969).

18. Victor Turner, *The Anthropology of Performance* (New York: Performing Arts Journal Publications, 1992), 24.

19. D. H. Mellor, *Real Time* (Cambridge: Cambridge University Press, 1981).

20. Alfred Gell, *The Anthropology of Time* (Oxford: Berg Publishers, 1992).

21. Ibid.

22. Edmund Husserl, *The Phenomenology of Internal Time Consciousness,* trans. J. S. Churchill (Bloomington: Indiana University Press, 1964), 43.

23. Gell, *The Anthropology of Time,* 222.

24. Ibid.

25. For further details of Husserl's analysis of temporal perception, see Husserl, *The Phenomenology of Internal Time Consciousness,* and D. Welton, *The Essential Husserl: Basic Writings in Transcendental Phenomenology* (Bloomington: Indiana University Press, 1999).

26. Gell, *The Anthropology of Time.*

27. Alfred Gell, "The Language of the Forest: Landscape and Phonological Iconism in Umeda," in *The Anthropology of Landscape*, ed. Eric Hirsh and Michael O'Hanlon (Oxford: Clarendon Press, 1995), 238–39.

28. Victor Zuckerkandl, *Sound and Symbol* (London: Routledge and Kegan Paul, 1956).

29. Hans Meyerhoff, *Time in Literature* (Berkeley: University of California Press, 1968).

30. Ibid., 21–22.

31. Zuckerkandl, *Sound and Symbol*, 206.

32. Ibid., 233.

33. Ibid., 151.

34. Ibid., 185.

35. Rural inhabitants of North Potosi, near the border with Oruro.

36. Olivia Harris, "The Dead and the Devils among the Bolivian Laymi," in *Death and the Regeneration of Life*, ed. M. Bloch and J. Parry (Cambridge: Cambridge University Press, 1982).

37. Harris, "The Dead and the Devils among the Bolivian Laymi."

38. Ibid., 59.

39. In an appendix to his book *The Masked Media*, Hans Buechler states that, on the contrary, in Irpa Chico (a community near La Paz) the tarka was played when too much rain was falling because its hoarse sound was considered to attract dry spells—Hans Buechler, *The Masked Media: Aymara Fiestas and Social Interaction in the Bolivian Highlands* (The Hague: Mouton Publishers, 1980).

40. Harris, "The Dead and the Devils among the Bolivian Laymi," 60.

41. Henry Stobart, *Sounding the Seasons: Music Ideologies and the Poetics of Production in an Andean Hamlet*. (PhD diss., University of Cambridge, 1996).

42. The information was obtained from the statistic charts of the Asociación de Conjuntos del Folklore de Oruro (the institution in charge of organizing the Carnival parade). Although the number of brass bands and musicians are specified in the documents, they do not provide detailed accounts of the traditional instruments.

43. I interviewed this musician in August 2000, but I have changed his name to protect his anonymity.

44. Juan Carlos Estenssoro, "Modernismo, estética, música y fiesta: Elites y cambio de actitud frente a la cultura popular: Perú 1750–1850," in *Tradición y Modernidad en los Andes*, ed. H. Urbano (Cusco: Centro de Estudios Regionales Andinos Bartolomé de las Casas, 1992).

45. Juan Carlos Estenssoro, *Música y sociedad coloniales: Lima 1680–1830* (Lima: Editorial Colmillo Blanco, 1989).

46. Estenssoro, "Modernismo, estética, música y fiesta."

47. Ibid., 181.

48. I believe Buechler refers here to people who return from the cities to their communities of origin rather than to the "mixed blood" people generally referred to as mestizos. Due to spatial limitations in this chapter, I cannot develop a discussion of social stratification here (see Araoz, *Heavenly and Grotesque Imageries [Re]created in the Carnival of Oruro, Bolivia*).

49. Buechler, *The Masked Media*, 379.

50. These bands usually play Morenadas, Diabladas, and other rhythms of the local Carnival, apart from the popular Latin American cumbia and salsa.

51. Leach, *Replanteamiento de la Antropología*.

52. There are, for example, several blocks of dance groups—each block divisible into groups and each group divisible into smaller sections—that follow an order established by the institution in charge of organizing the events, the Asociación de Conjuntos del Folklore de Oruro.

53. Zuckerkandl, *Sound and Symbol*.

54. *Alba* means "dawn," and it is interpreted as a greeting to the sun. Some say it is also a greeting to Venus, the morning star.

55. For an analysis of the spatial enactment of the Alba rite, see Araoz, *Heavenly and Grotesque Imageries (Re)created in the Carnival of Oruro, Bolivia*.

56. Husserl, *The Phenomenology of Internal Time Consciousness;* Zuckerkandl, *Sound and Symbol*.

57. According to a famous embroidery specialist, the Moreno costume weighs between twenty and thirty kilograms.

58. Xavier Albó and Matías Preiswerk, *Los Señores del Gran Poder* (La Paz: Centro de Teología Popular, Taller de Observaciones Culturales, 1986), 64. (The translation is my own.)

59. According to the official ACFO magazine for Carnival 1997, Oruro.

60. J. Murillo Vacarreza, *La Danza del Moreno*. Essay included within the documents presented by the *Fraternidad Morenada Central Oruro, fundada por la Comunidad Cocanis* to the ACFO, Oruro, 1980.

61. For further details on this dance, see Vacarreza, *La Danza del Moreno*, and Araoz, *Heavenly and Grotesque Imageries (Re)created in the Carnival of Oruro, Bolivia*.

62. Anthony Seeger, *Why Suya Sing: A Musical Anthropology of an Amazonian People* (Cambridge: Cambridge University Press, 1987).

63. Araoz, *Heavenly and Grotesque Imageries (Re)created in the Carnival of Oruro, Bolivia.*

7. Such a Noise! Fireworks and the Soundscapes of Two Veracruz Festivals

Epigraph: Katherine Anne Porter, *Ship of Fools* (Boston: Atlantic Monthly Books, 1945), 13.

1. Dotz, Mingo, and Moyer write about childhood memories and mention that in the 1930s, Michigan was one of the first states to ban firecrackers. See Warren Dotz, Jack Mingo, and George Moyer, *Firecrackers: The Art and History* (Berkeley, CA: Ten Speed Press, 2004), 43–47.

2. Works on sound in history and, in particular, on the themes of time, order/disorder, commemoration, and modernity include: David Cressy, *Bonfires and Bells: National Memory and the Protestant Calendar in Elizabethan and Stuart England* (London: Sutton, 2004); Richard Cullen Rath, *How Early America Sounded* (Ithaca, NY: Cornell University Press, 2003); Mark M. Smith, *Sensing the Past: Seeing, Hearing, Smelling, Tasting and Touching in History* (Berkeley: University of California Press, 2007); Júnia Ferreira Furtado, "Os sons e os silêncios nas minas de ouro," in *Sons, formas, cores e movimientos na modernidade Atlântica: Europa, Américas e África,* ed. Júnia Ferreira Furtado (São Paulo: Annablume, 2008), 19–56.

3. On Carnival in Veracruz, see Martha Inés Cortés Rodríguez, *Máscaras: Los espectáculos teatrales en Veracruz (1873–1975), El carnival de Veracruz en 1867* (Veracruz: Instituto Veracruzano de Cultura, 1990); Martha Inés Cortés Rodríguez, *Los carnavales en Veracruz* (Veracruz: Instituto Veracruzano de Cultura, 2000); Horacio Guadarrama Olivera, "Los carnavales del Puerto de Veracruz," in *La Habana/Veraruz, Veracruz/La Habana: Las dos orillas,* eds. Bernardo García Díaz and Sergio Guerra Vilaboy (Xalapa: Universidad Veracruzana/Universidad de Habana, 2002); Guido Munch Garrido, *Una semblanza del carnaval de Veracruz* (Mexico City: UNAM, 2004); Juan Antonio Flores Martos, "El carnaval veracruzano, disciplinas, singularidad y política de la cultural popular," in *La fiesta en el mundo hispánico,* eds. Palma Martínez-Burgos García and Alfredo Rodríguez González (Cuenca: Ediciones de la universidad de Castilla-La Mancha, 2004), 107–44; Juan Antonio Flores Martos, "Los encapuchados del carnaval del Puerto de Veracruz: Una indagación etnográfica en la memoria cultural e imaginación urbana," *Sotavento: Revista de historia, sociedad y cultura,* no. 4, (Summer 1998): 57–115; Andrew Grant Wood, "Introducing La reina del carnaval: Public Celebration and Postrevolutionary Discourse in Veracruz, Mexico," in *Americas: A Quarterly Review of In-*

ter-American Cultural History 60, no. 1 (2003): 87–108; Andrew Grant Wood, *Carnival in Veracruz: An Illustrated History* (unpublished manuscript). For Carnival in Mexico, see Haydée Quiroz Malca, *El carnaval en México: Abanico de culturas* (Mexico City: CONACULTA, 2002). On Candelaria, see Ricardo Pérez Montfort, *Tlacotalpan: La virgen, la candelaria y los sones* (Mexico City: Fondo de Cultura Económica, 1996); Antonio García de León, *Fandango: El ritual del mundo jarocho a través los siglos* (Mexico City: CONACULTA, 2006).

4. The idea of fire as a medium conjures many possible fruitful connections, ranging from agricultural strategies and tactics to cooking and, ultimately, the rise of civilization. On fire, see, for example, Stephen J. Pyne, *Fire: A Brief History* (Seattle: University of Washington Press, 2004). Other related works include Alan St. H. Brock, *A History of Fireworks* (London: George G. Harrap, 1949); J. R. Parrington, *A History of Greek Fire and Gunpowder* (Cambridge: W. Heffer and Sons, 1960); Kevin Salatino, *Incendiary Art: The Representation of Fireworks in Early Modern Europe* (Los Angeles: Getty Publishers, 1998); George Plimpton, *Fireworks* (New York: Doubleday, 1984); Dotz, Mingo, and Moyer, *Firecrackers.*

5. Dotz, Mingo, and Moyer, *Firecrackers*, 36.

6. Brock, *A History of Fireworks.*

7. Dotz, Mingo, and Moyer, *Firecrackers,* 51–53.

8. Brock, *A History of Fireworks,* 129–32.

9. Francis Scott Key originally wrote these lines in 1814 after watching British ships attack Fort McHenry on the Chesapeake Bay during the War of 1812.

10. Not surprisingly, when uncertain social or economic conditions arise, celebratory public events such as Independence Day rituals duly reflect those changes—both in how they are produced (i.e., shorter displays, longer intervals between bursts, and even cancellations due to tightened budgets) and in the myriad ways observers interpret and reflect upon the meaning of official ritual discourse. Given economic hard times, the city of Houston, Texas, nevertheless spent $850,000 on its massive fireworks production in 2009, which was approximately half the amount spent the previous year. Other cities with less available money have simply canceled local celebrations. See "With Budgets Tight, Less Flash for the Fourth," *New York Times,* July 2, 2009.

11. Paul Hegarty, *Noise/Music: A History* (New York: Continuum Books, 2008), 124.

12. Néstor García Canclini, *Transforming Modernity: Popular Culture in Mexico* (Austin: University of Texas Press, 1993), 101.

13. Stanley Brandes, *Power and Persuasion: Fiestas and Social Control in Rural Mexico* (Philadelphia: University of Pennsylvania Press, 1988), 125.

14. Linda Curcio-Nagy notes the use of firecrackers in Mexico City as a means of celebrating the king. Linda Curcio-Nagy, *The Great Festivals of Colonial Mexico City: Performing Power and Identity* (Albuquerque: University of New Mexico Press, 2004), 105. She writes that in 1780, a vice regal decree sought to stimulate the use of pyrotechnics in festival celebrations. With the government holding a monopoly on the sale of gunpowder, this added revenue to government coffers and allegedly provided jobs for commoners involved in the production of firecrackers.

15. Frances Toor, *A Treasury of Mexican Folkways* (New York: Bonanza Books, 1947), 171. For a listing of Carnival celebrations throughout Mexico (and the widespread use of fireworks), see Haydée Quiroz Malca, *El carnival en México*, 155–77. Similarly, for Semana Santa (Holy Week), see Sonia C. Iglesias y Cabrera, Leticia Salazar Cárdenas, and Julio César Martínez Gómez, *La semana santa en México: Con la muerte en la cruz* (Mexico City: CONACULTA, 2002), 97–104. For various religious brotherhoods and patron saint celebrations, see Dubravka Mindek, *Fiestas de gremios ayer y hoy* (Mexico City: CONACULTA, 2001), 47–53. On Judas burnings, see William H. Beezley, *Judas at the Jockey Club and Other Episodes of Porfirian Mexico* (Lincoln: University of Nebraska Press, 1987). Given their seeming ubiquity in public life, fireworks have strangely not received much attention by scholars of Mexico. There are a few exceptions, however, such as Stanley Brandes, who focused on celebrations in Tzintzuntzan, Michoacán; Harvey Goldberg, who has written on the famous *barrio de los coheteros* (El Cerrillo neighborhood) in San Cristobal de las Casas; and Gabriel Angelotti Pasteur, who observed fireworks construction and distribution in Halachó, Yucatán. Others, such as anthropologist Evon Z. Vogt and historian Antonio García de León, include a discussion of fireworks usage in a larger consideration of community and regional ritual practice. Harvey Goldberg, *The Coheteros of San Cristobal* (Cambridge, MA: Harvard Summer Field Studies, 1961); Brandes, *Power and Persuasion;* Gabriel Angelotti Pasteur, *Artesanía prohibida: De cómo lo tradicional se convierte en clandestino* (Mexico City: Instituto Nacional de Antropología y Historia/El Colegio de Michoacán/Universidad Autónoma de Yucatán, 2004); Evon Z. Vogt, *Tortillas for the Gods: A Symbolic Analysis of Zinacanteco Rituals* (Cambridge, MA: Harvard University Press, 1976); Antonio García de León, ed., *Fandango: El ritual del mundo jarocho a través los siglos.* In addition to describing fireworks displays, scholars have noted how villages save all year for their patron saint day celebration. In San Cristobal, a nine-day festival in late July and early August dedicated to El señor de la transfiguración includes regular use of locally produced skyrockets.

Both Brandes and Angelotti Pasteur write extensively about the social context in which fireworks are produced.

16. Probably the most comprehensive description of fireworks construction can be found in Brock, *A History of Fireworks*, 181–254. Alan St. H. Brock's father, Frank Arthur Brock, was a British Air Force officer who invented the smoke screen, which was used toward the end of World War I. He died in combat in 1918.

17. George Plimpton's brief survey of fireworks around the world at the end of his book includes a short bit on castillos, cascadas, and cohetes in Mexico. Plimpton, *Fireworks*, 245–47.

18. Brandes, *Power and Persuasion*, 113.

19. Ibid.

20. Interview with Margarita de la Cruz de la Angel, Veracruz, June 23, 2006.

21. Archivo Municipal del Puerto de Veracruz, Civif 21–23 (1610 Mandamiento del virrey Luis de Velasco, dirigido al Corregidor de la Veracruz, que prohibe el uso de fuegos artificiales); Civifs 23–24 (1610 Mandamiento del virrey marqués de Salinas, para que el Corregidor de la Veracruz cumpla con la prohibición relativea al uso de fuegos artificiales); Civif 24 (1611 Pregón en la plaza pública de la Veracruz a la prohibición de fuegos artificiales). See also Margarita de la Cruz del Angel et al., *Catálogo de documentos coloniales, 1608–1810: Archivo Histórico de la Ciudad de Veracruz* (Veracruz: H. Ayuntamiento de Veracruz Archivo Histórico de la Ciudad de Veracruz/Secretaría de Gobernación Archivo General de la Nación, 1993). Personal communication with María del Rosario Ochoa Rivera, September 20, 2006.

22. Martha Poblett Miranda, *Cien viajeros en Veracruz: Crónicas y relatos* (Xalapa: Gobierno del Estado de Veracruz, 1992), VII:169.

23. Miranda, *Cien Viajeros en Veracruz*, VIII:336.

24. Ibid., 357.

25. Ralph Lee Woodward, *Here and There in Mexico: The Travel Writings of Mary Ashley Townsend* (Tuscaloosa: University of Alabama Press, 2001), 120.

26. I was so impressed with Townsend's playfully descriptive language that I decided to use an extended extract for the title of an earlier version of this chapter. "Such a noise! Such whizzing, and fizzing, and shooting, and floods of fire and avalanches of sparks and everything apparently going in an opposite direction to everything else all at the same time!" Paper presented at the XII Meeting of Canadian, U.S. and Mexican Historians of Mexico, Vancouver, Canada, October 2006. At one point in the presentation, I encouraged histori-

ans to return to the old practice of utilizing long titles for their published work. Although I was dead serious, most attendees just laughed.

27. Miranda, *Cien Viajeros en Veracruz*, XI:26–27.

28. Ibid., 65.

29. George Summerlin to Secretary of State, April 27, 1922. U.S. Department of State records pertaining to the internal affairs of Mexico, 1910–1929, Reel 161.

30. *El Dictamen*, May 2, 1922.

31. On the history of the tenant movement, see Andrew Grant Wood, *Revolution in the Street: Women, Workers and Urban Protest in Veracruz, 1870–1927* (Wilmington, DE: SR Books/Roman and Littlefield, 2001).

32. Wood, *Revolution in the Street,* 141.

33. Ibid., 155.

34. Ibid., 159–60.

35. Ibid., 158.

36. *El Dictamen*, February 7, 1925.

37. For an overview of the pre-Lenten festival in Mexico, see Haydée Quiroz Malca, *El carnaval en México: Abanico de culturas.*

38. On the history of tourism in Veracruz, see Andrew Grant Wood, "On the Selling of Rey Momo: Early Tourism and the Marketing of Carnival in Veracruz," in *Holiday in Mexico: Essays on Tourism and Tourist Encounters,* eds. Dina Berger and Andrew Grant Wood (Durham, NC: Duke University Press, 2010), 77–106.

39. Martha Cortés, *Los carnavales en Veracruz*, 31, 45.

40. On the early history of modern Carnival, see Andrew Grant Wood, "Introducing *La reina del Carnaval,*" 87–108.

41. Rosario Ochoa, personal communication, Veracruz, Mexico, September 14, 2006.

42. Not surprisingly, many church officials take a dim view of Carnival. Still, one has to appreciate the near–mirror imaging of the celebration's ritual structure as a complement to Christian doctrine, not to mention the anticipation of Lent.

43. *El Dictamen*, February 26, 1925.

44. A young person's blog on Yahoo.com I discovered recently asks why fireworks were banned in Veracruz. Various responses debated issues of safety as contrasted with one's individual right to enjoy a good firecracker fiesta every once and a while. As the lead response, "Ingrid" claimed that in "Veracruz many people have died in firework related accidents . . . not to mention the fact that

they are very dangerous for kids to play with" (http://mx.answers.yahoo.com /question/index?qid=20060910113715AAYg9mG). Judging from a number of Mexican newspaper reports during the last ten years, there is little doubt that many people have been hurt in fireworks-related accidents. Two examples in recent history include seventeen dead and twenty-five injured in an explosion in Tultepec on October 14, 1998, and fifty-six dead in Celaya on September 27, 1997. Pasteur, *Artesanía prohibida*, 230.

45. On Candelaria, as part of the larger regional cultural (and particularly musical) scene, see, for example, Antonio García de León, *Fandango: El ritual del mundo jarocho a través los siglos*. In part, the book contains a selection of primary documents, including a variety of travel writings. The text also includes excerpts (some describing Candelaria) from the Jáltiban-based reporter "Epalocho" (Eulogio Aguirre Santiesteban), whose detailed dispatches were published in *La Opinión* during the 1930s and 1940s. In 1998, when the town became a UNESCO World Heritage Site, the international body identified the town's built environment as "represent[ing] a fusion of Spanish and Caribbean traditions of exceptional importance and quality." Further, their statement qualified the town because of its "wide streets, modest houses in a variety of styles and colors, and many mature trees in public and private open spaces" (UNESCO, 1998, http://whc.unesco.org/en/list/862).

46. The year 2010 marked the thirty-first year of the music festival.

47. In 2010, Candelaria extended for eleven days.

48. Hugo A. Rennert, *The Spanish Stage at the Time of Lope de Vega* (New York: Dover, 1963), 295–96.

49. Many of these appearing in 2006 closely resembled the still hugely disgraced former president Carlos Salinas de Gotari. His *sexenio* (term limit for Mexican presidents) extended from December 1988 to November 1994.

50. Ricardo Pérez Montfort, *Tlacotalpan: La virgen, la candelaria y los sones* (Mexico City: Fondo de Cultura Económica, 1996), 144.

51. Agustín Lara (1897–1970) was a famed bolero composer and musician thought to be a native son of Tlacotalpan, despite his being born in Mexico City. See Andrew Grant Wood, *Agustín Lara: A Cultural Biography* (New York: Oxford University Press, 2012).

52. Brandes, *Power and Persuasion*, 110.

Postscript. Sound Representation: Nation, Translation, Memory

1. James Lastra, *Sound Technology and the American Cinema* (New York: Columbia University Press, 2000), 137.

2. Rudolf Arnheim, *Radio* (London: Faber and Faber, 1936), 238.

3. Michel-Rolph Trouillot, *Silencing the Past: Power and the Production of History* (Boston: Beacon Press, 1995), 26.

4. Jonathan Sterne, "Preserving Sound in Modern America," in *Hearing History: A Reader,* ed. Mark M. Smith (Athens: University of Georgia Press, 2002), 296.

Contributors

Gonzalo Araoz studied arts and architecture at Miami Dade Community College (USA) and anthropology at the La Paz UMSA University (Bolivia), and he completed a PhD in social anthropology at the University of St Andrews (UK). His doctoral dissertation explored the depiction of grotesque realism in the Oruro Carnival. He is currently a research fellow at the University of Cumbria, where he founded the Transatlantic Research and Development Network on Mental Health and the Arts (www.tramha.org). He also leads the project Probing the Boundaries of Madness for the Interdisciplinary Network in Oxford, UK (www.inter-disciplinary.net/probing-the-boundaries /making-sense-of/madness).

Alejandra Bronfman completed her PhD in history at Princeton University in 2000. She is currently an associate professor in the Department of History at the University of British Columbia in Canada. Her book *Measures of Equality: Social Science, Citizenship and Race in Cuba, 1902–1940*, centered on the histories of social science and race in Cuba. She is also the author of *On the Move: The Caribbean Since 1989*, a recent history of the Caribbean with a particular focus on the circulation of goods, information, and people. Her current research project, "Talking Machines: Histories of Sound, Violence and Technology in the Caribbean," records the unwritten histories of radio and related sonic technologies in the Caribbean.

Gisela Cramer is an associate professor with the Department of History at the Universidad Nacional de Colombia in Bogotá. She has published on topics related to the political economy of Latin America and is currently working on the history of Nelson A. Rockefeller's Office of Inter-American Affairs (1940–1946).

Christine Ehrick earned her PhD at the University of California, Los Angeles. She is an associate professor of history at the University of Louisville in Kentucky. Her first book, *The Shield of the Weak: Feminism and the State in Uruguay, 1903–1933*, was published in 2005 by the University of New Mexico Press. She is currently completing a manuscript on women/gender and radio broadcasting in Buenos Aires, Argentina, and Montevideo, Uruguay, during the 1930s and 1940s. An essay entitled "Savage Dissonance: Gender, Voice, and Women's Radio Speech in Argentina, 1930–1945" appears in *Sound in the Era of Mechanical Reproduction*, edited by David Suisman and Susan Strasser and published in 2009 by the University of Pennsylvania Press.

Michele Hilmes is a professor of media and cultural studies and chair of the Department of Communication Arts at the University of Wisconsin-Madison. Her publications include *Radio Voices: American Broadcasting 1922–1952; Only Connect: A Cultural History of Broadcasting in the United States*; and *Network Nations: A Transnational History of British and American Broadcasting*.

Alejandro L. Madrid is associate professor and director of graduate studies in the Latin American and Latino studies program at the University of Illinois at Chicago. He is the author of *Nor-tec Rifa! Electronic Dance Music from Tijuana to the World* and *Sounds of the Modern Nation: Music, Culture and Ideas in Post-Revolutionary Mexico*. He is also editor of *Transnational Encounters: Music and Performance at the U.S.–Mexico Border* and coeditor of *Postnational Musical Identities: Cultural Production, Distribution and Consumption in a Globalized Scenario*. A recipient of the Woody Guthrie Book Award from the International Association for the Study of Popular Music–U.S. Branch (2010), the Casa de las Américas Award for Latin American Musicology (2005), the Samuel Claro Valdés Award for Latin American Musicology (2002), and the

A-R Editions Award of the American Musicological Society, Midwest Chapter (2001–2002), Madrid serves on the advisory boards of the *Latin American Music Review*; *Dancecult: Journal of Electronic Dance Music Culture;* and *Trans. Revista Transcultural de Música*, the editorial advisory board for the music collection of Editorial Doble J, and the international advisory board of the Tepoztlán Institute for the Transnational History of the Americas. He is also senior editor of Latin American and Latina/o entries for the new edition of the *Grove Dictionary of American Music*.

FERNANDO DE SOUSA ROCHA holds a PhD in comparative literature from the University of Southern California. His research focuses on Brazilian literary and cultural studies, particularly in relation to subaltern voices and the complex relationship between the lettered world and oral-auditory cultures. His most recent publication, about a New York–based performance by renowned Brazilian playwright Nelson Rodrigues, appeared in the *Luso-Brazilian Review*. He is currently an assistant professor of Portuguese at Middlebury College.

ANDREW GRANT WOOD earned his PhD in Latin American history from the University of California, Davis. Among his recent publications is a study of the life and times of Mexican popular composer Agustín Lara (Oxford University Press, 2012). He is a professor of history at the University of Tulsa.

INDEX